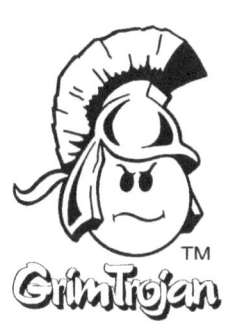

GrimTrojan™

The How-To Book for
Artists Who Can't Draw™

By Steven Moore

GRIM TROJAN™

www.grimtrojan.com

Grim Trojan–Loxley, AL

About this book—

I'm not going to say that everyone can learn to draw—I don't actually believe that. However, I do believe that most people—if they really want to—can learn to draw. Not everyone is going to be great at it, but if you are interested enough to devote the necessary time to learning, you should be able to develop good drawing skills.

This book is broken into two parts—a coloring book and a how-to draw workbook. Coloring is an art of its own. Not only can it be fun and relaxing, but an understanding of colors as well as improved eye-hand coordination can form in coloring.

If all you are interested in is coloring, I hope you enjoy the pictures I've included in this book. Though one typically tries to remain true to certain constants (blue sky—if it's a clear day, green leaves, yellow lemons, etc.) and attempts to keep the colors within the lines, often those who bend and/or break the rules create the most interesting art. Do you use all solid colors or do you shade and blend the colors? Crayons, color pencils or markers? It's entirely up to you. Have fun.

Those of you who wish to learn to draw—I recommend you also enjoy coloring a few of these pages before starting the how-to workbook part of the book. For you—as your instructor—I'm going to limit your options. I want you to take time to look at the art and apply the appropriate colors where they go in the picture. If it's an apple, make it red. If it's the trunk of a tree, make it brown. I want you to be paying attention to the art. Thinking about what color should go in each part of the picture will help you do that. Of course, blending shades and colors is entirely okay. The more time you put into studying the art and getting the colors where they belong the better. I also want you to make sure you stay in the lines. Even I have trouble with that when coloring, so don't be dismayed if you go out a little. Just do the best you can. The better you get at staying in the lines the better control you'll have over a pencil when you start to draw.

You don't have to color any of the pictures before moving onto the drawing part of this book, but I believe you would benefit from coloring at least a few pages.

For the workbook part of this book, you'll need a good pencil (I prefer technical/mechanical pencils because they maintain a nice sized edge, but you can use any pencil you are comfortable with—just be sure to keep a fairly sharp point on it). You'll do better if you don't work with pens or markers when drawing. Once you have a finished piece of art you can always go back and ink it. You'll need tracing paper or tracing vellum (technically tracing vellum is tracing paper, but the quality of vellum tends to be better. I'd recommend the vellum, however, tracing paper will work just fine). You should also get a drawing notebook/pad to sketch in when you're not using the workbook and to practice in outside of the pages provided in the book.

The most important part of working in this book is to have fun. If you're not enjoying yourself, you're doing something wrong.

Okay, let's get started...

Color a few of the coloring pages at the front of this book before beginning the drawing lessons. Be sure to color at least two or three pictures to work on your eye-hand coordination (and have fun while you're at it). Then you can move on to the instructions that follow the coloring section.

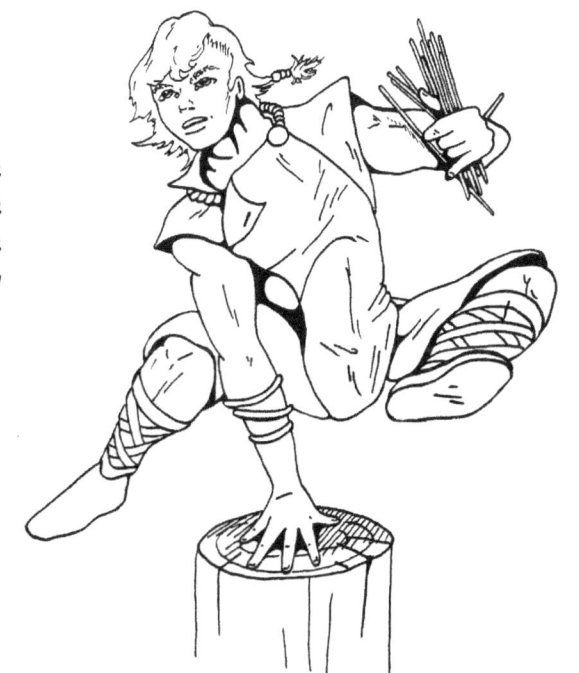

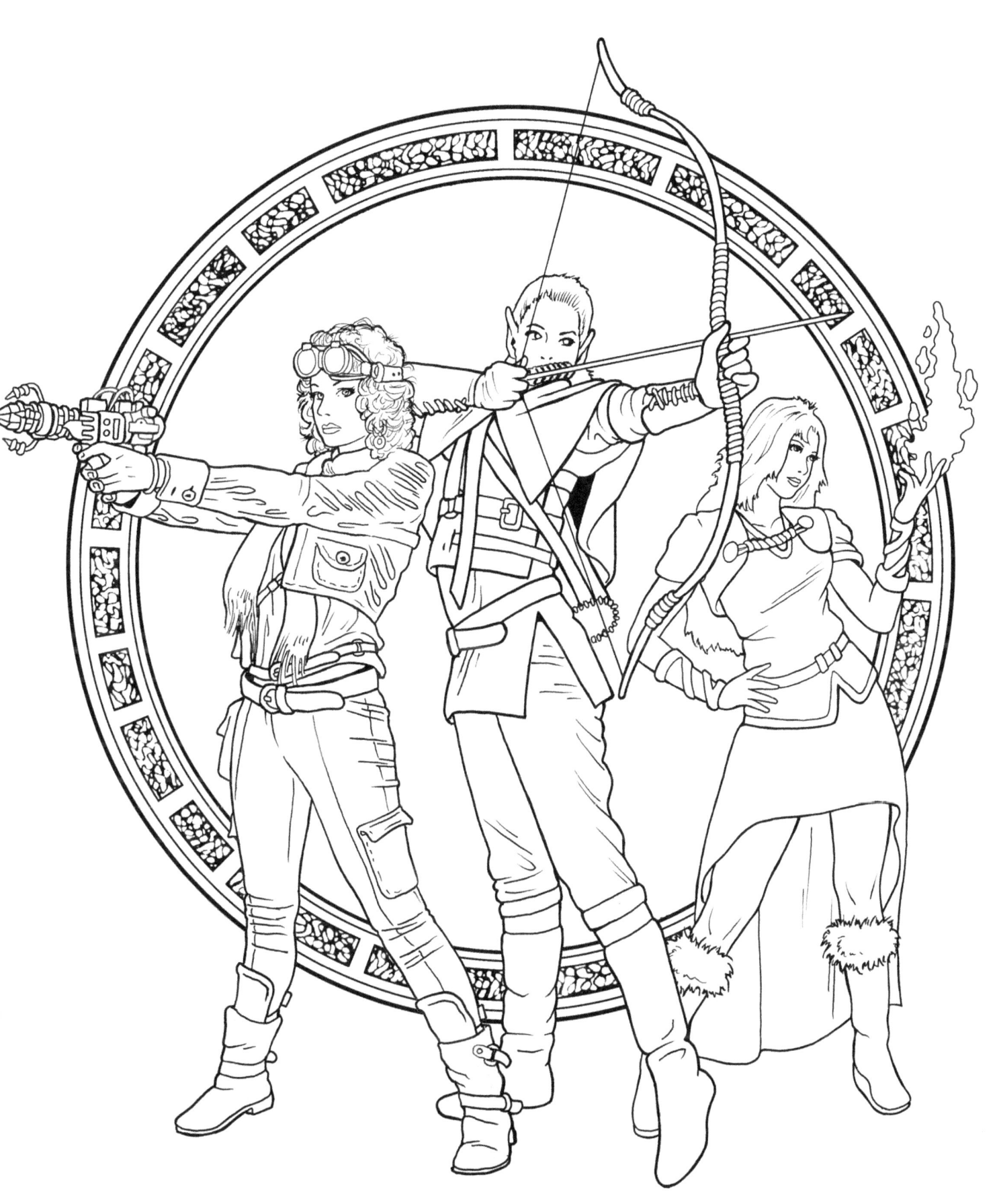

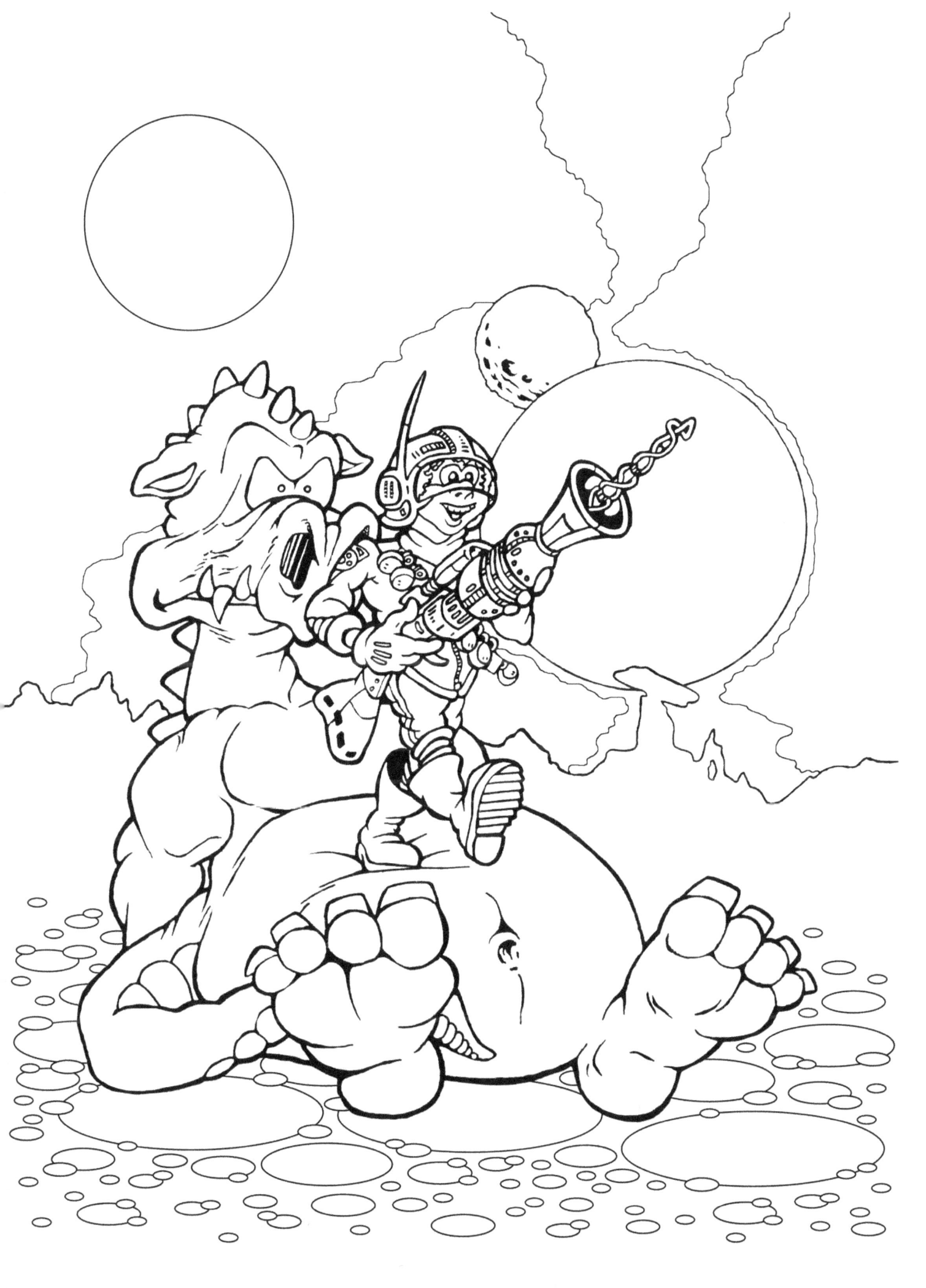

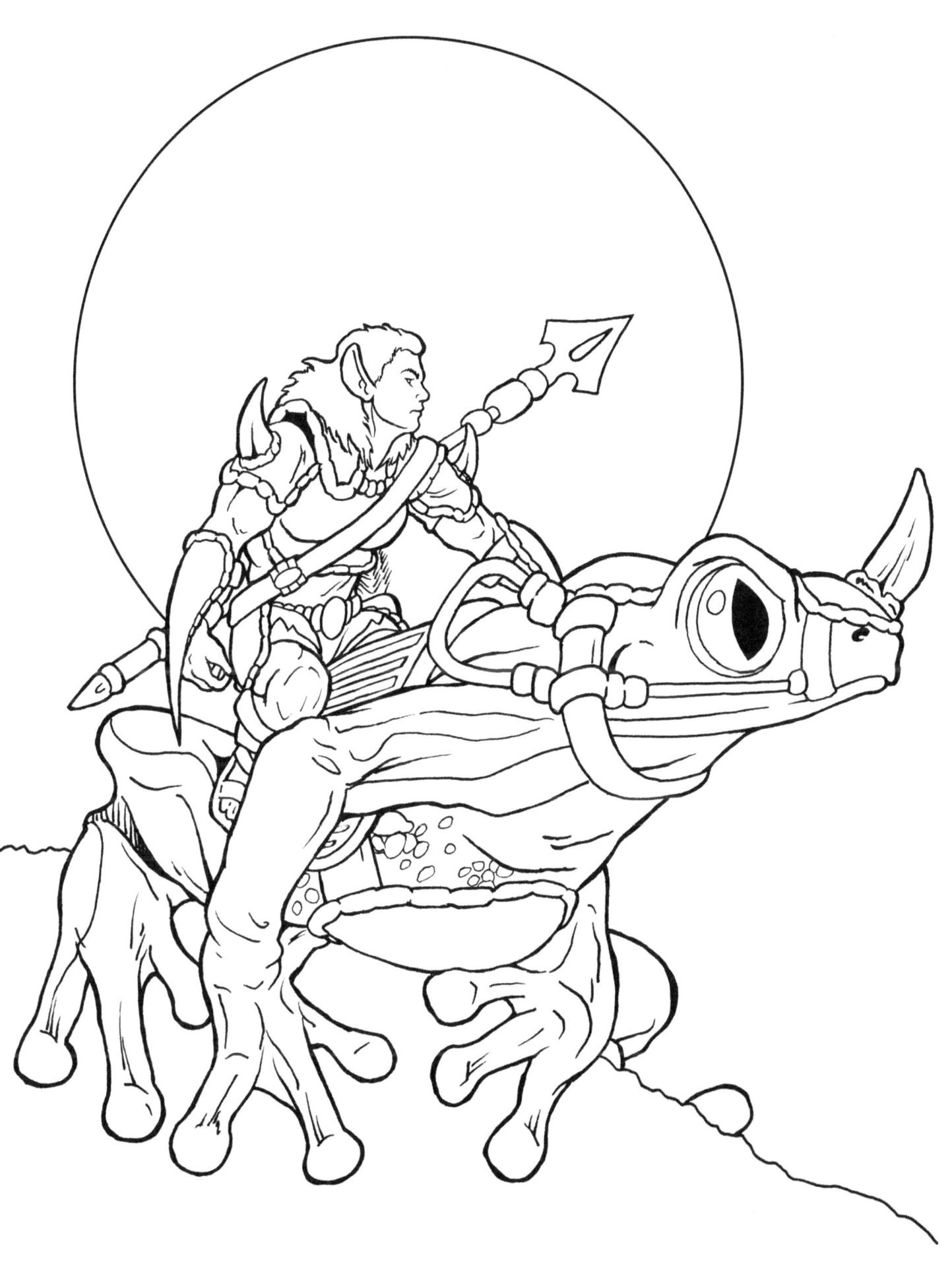

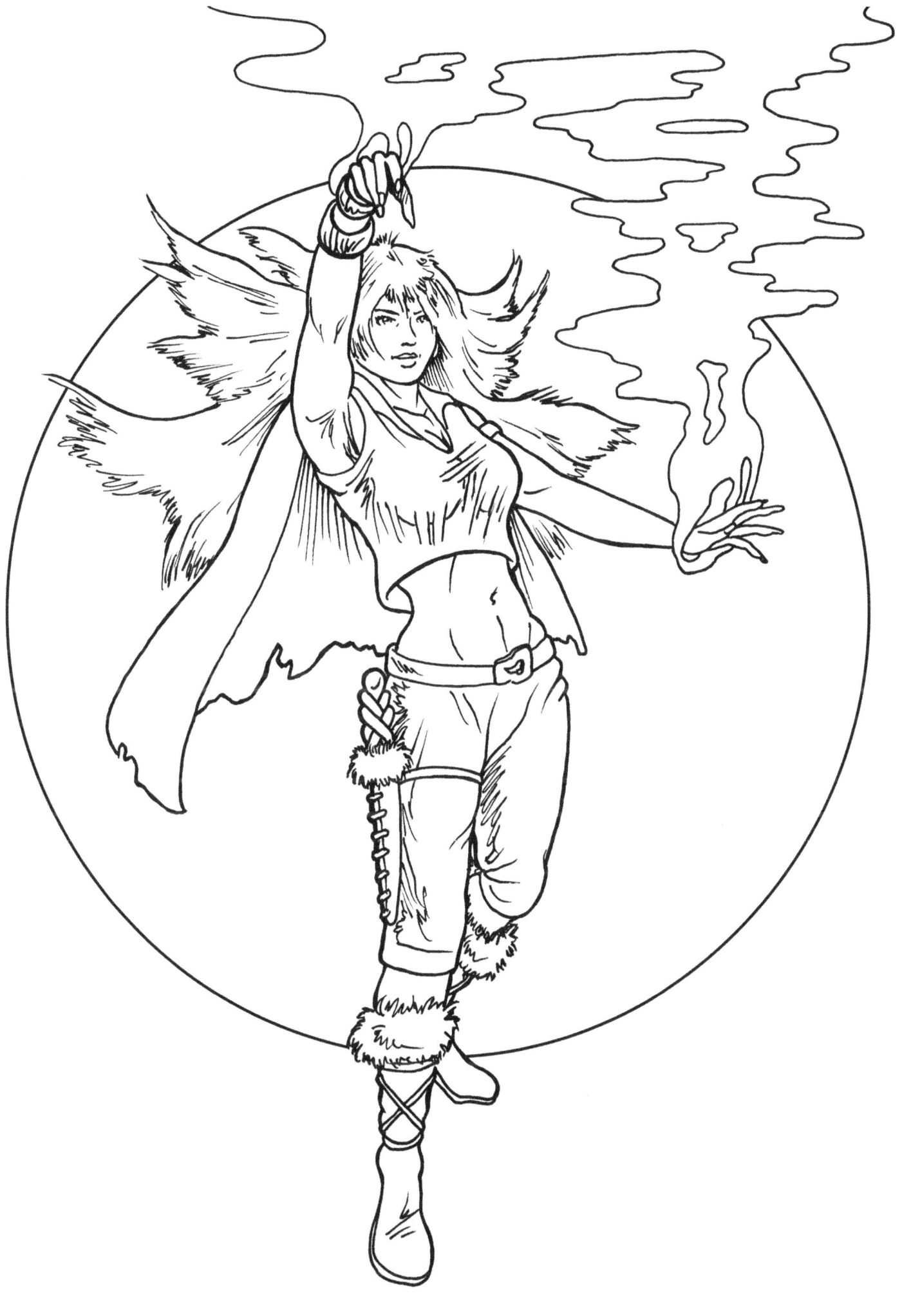

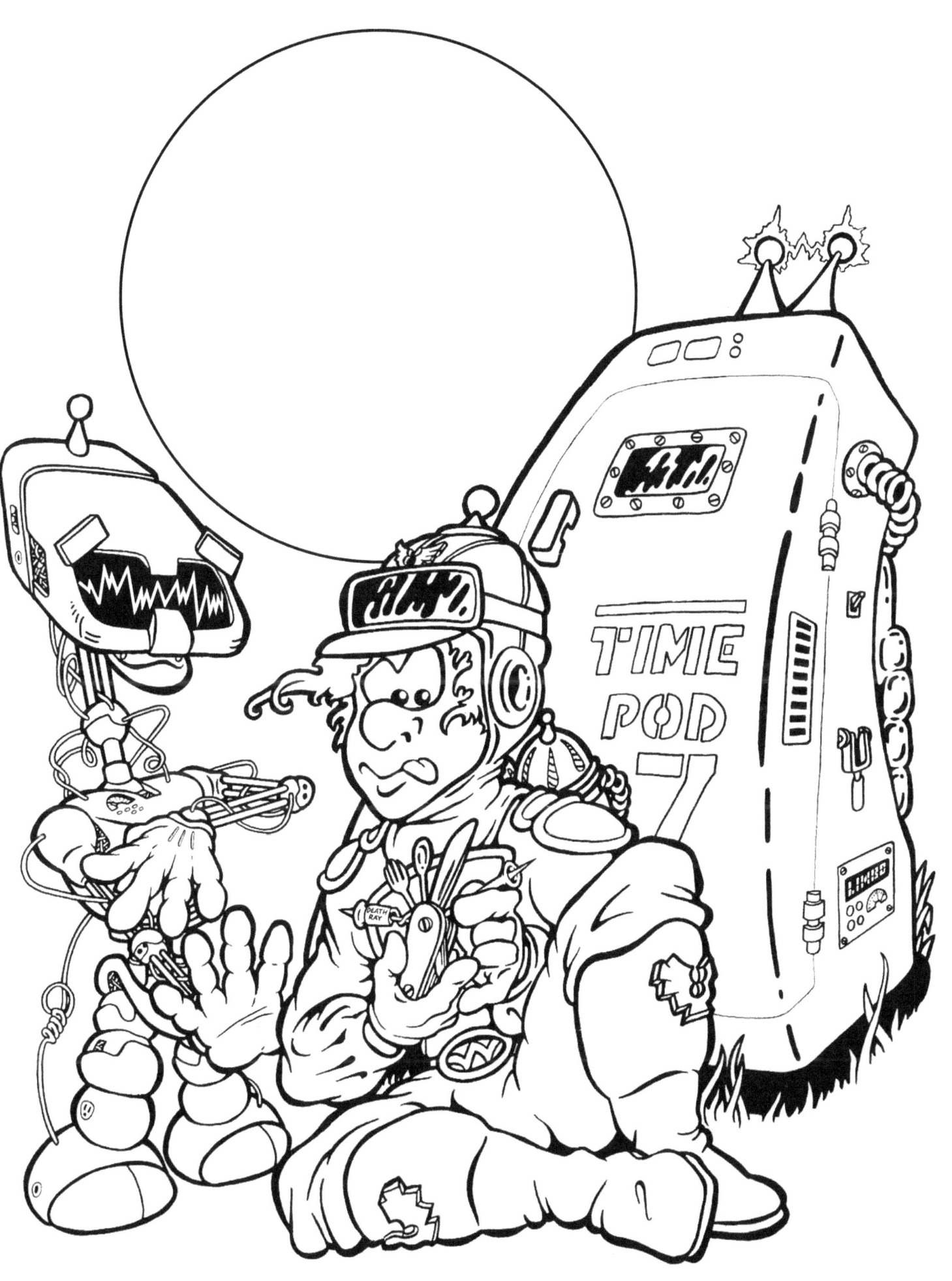

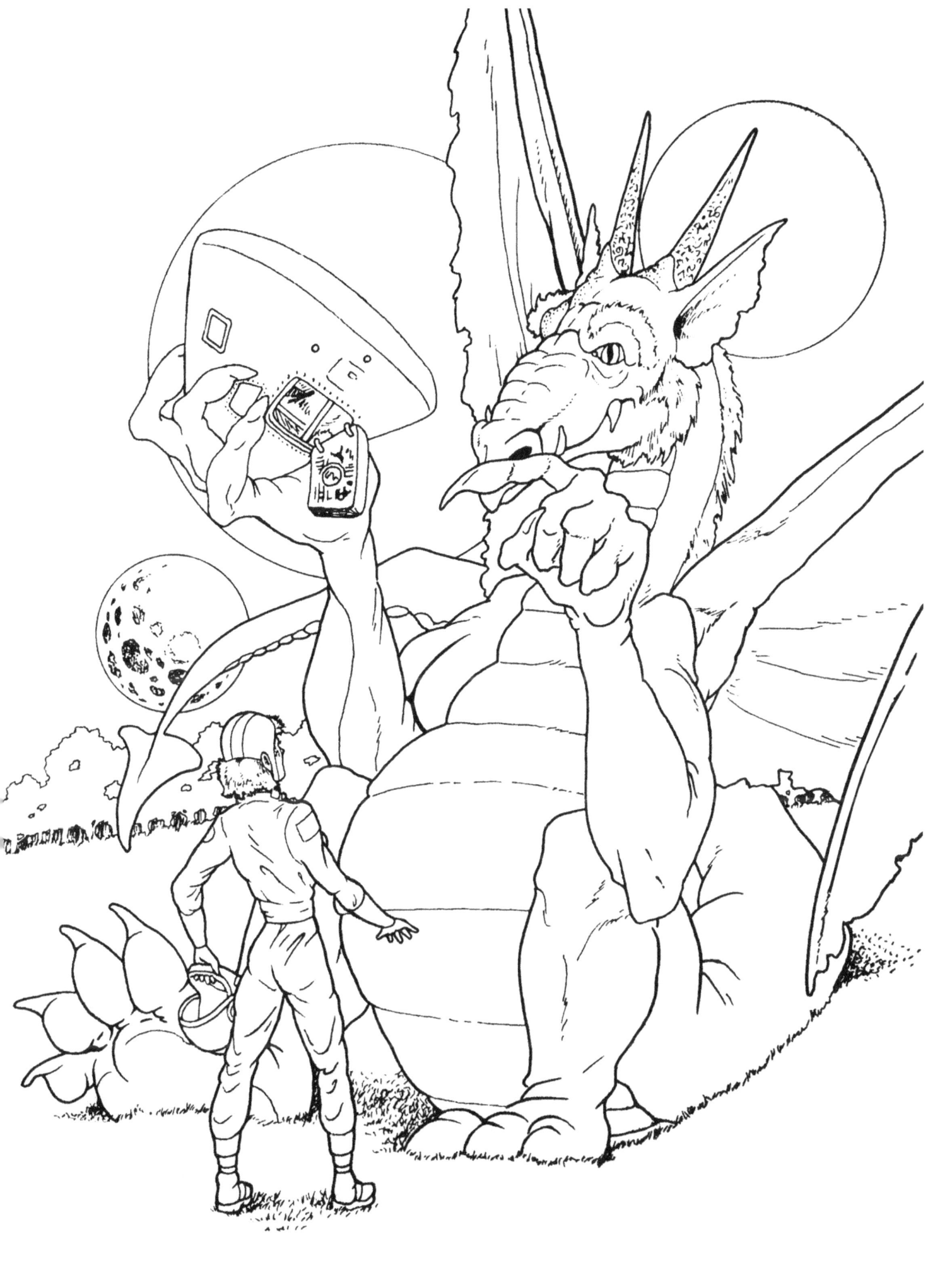

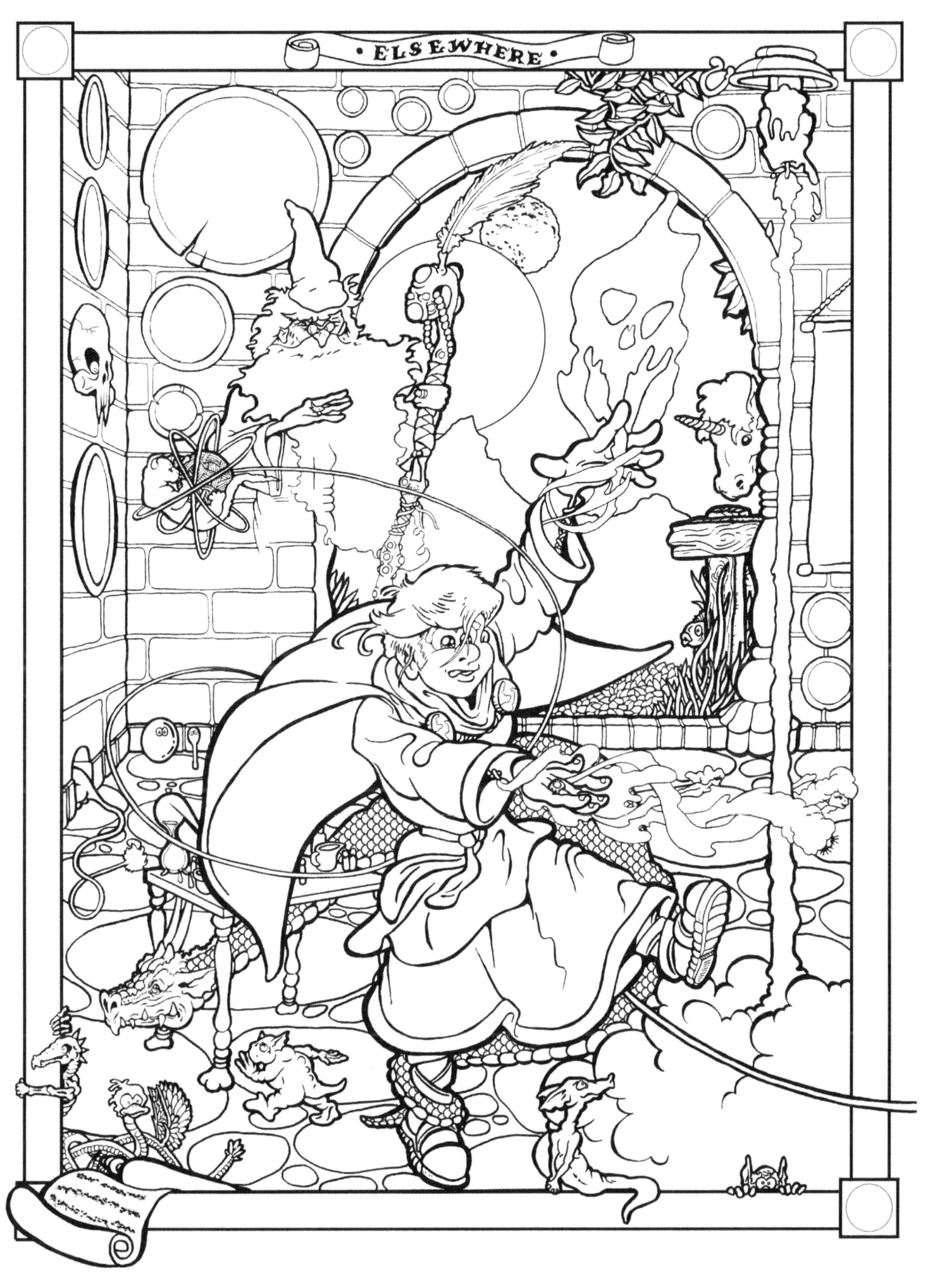

· ELSEWHERE ·

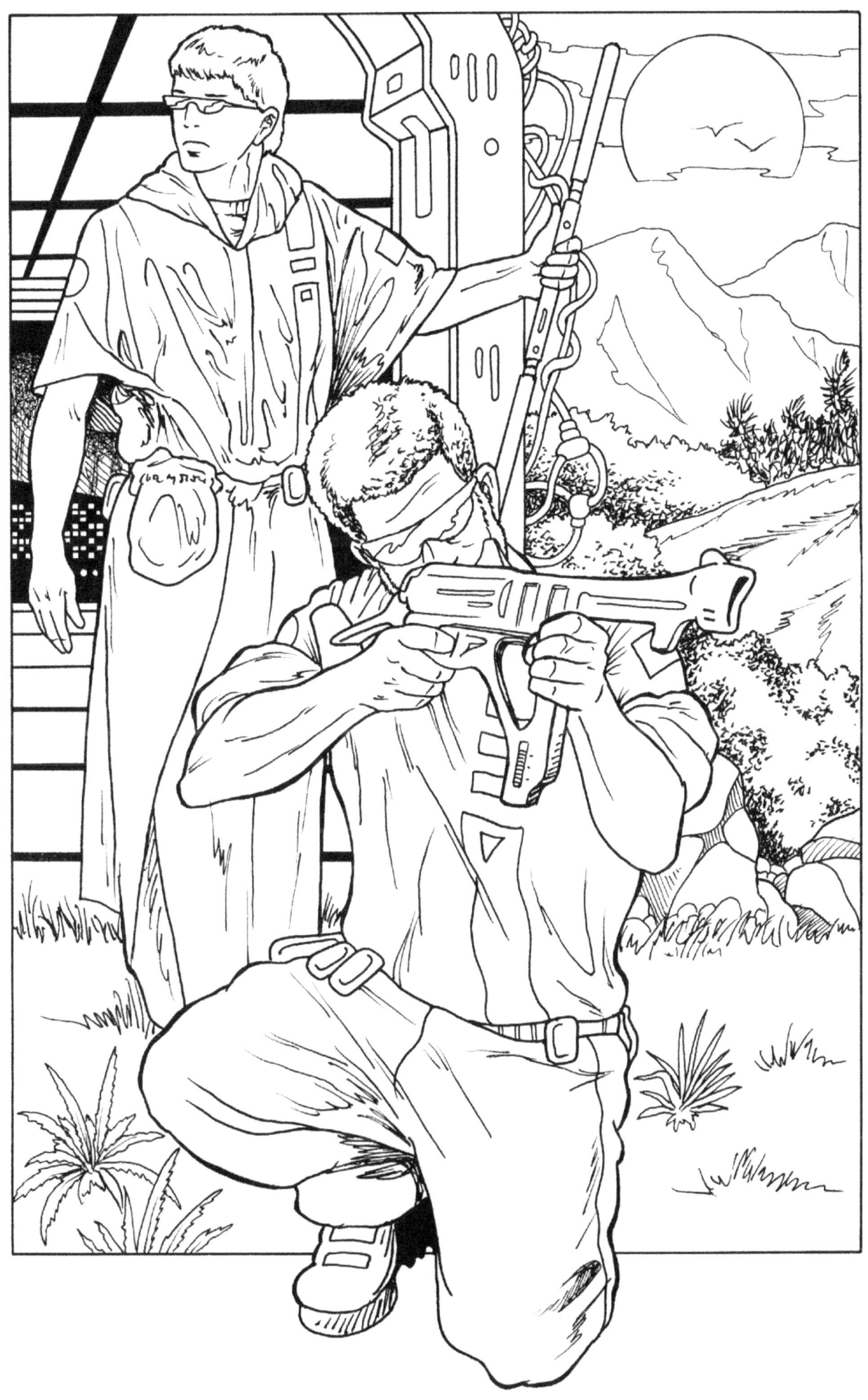

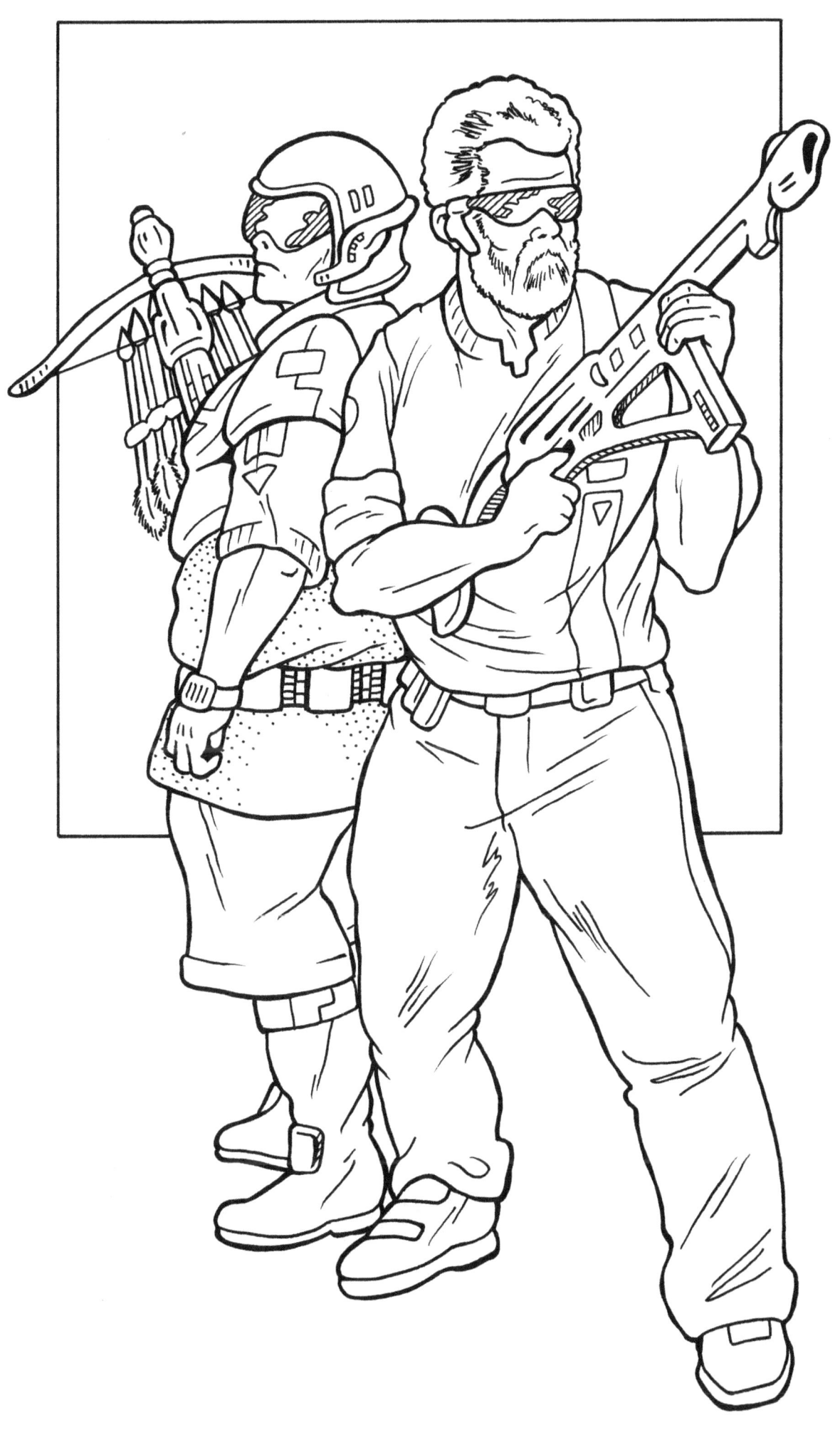

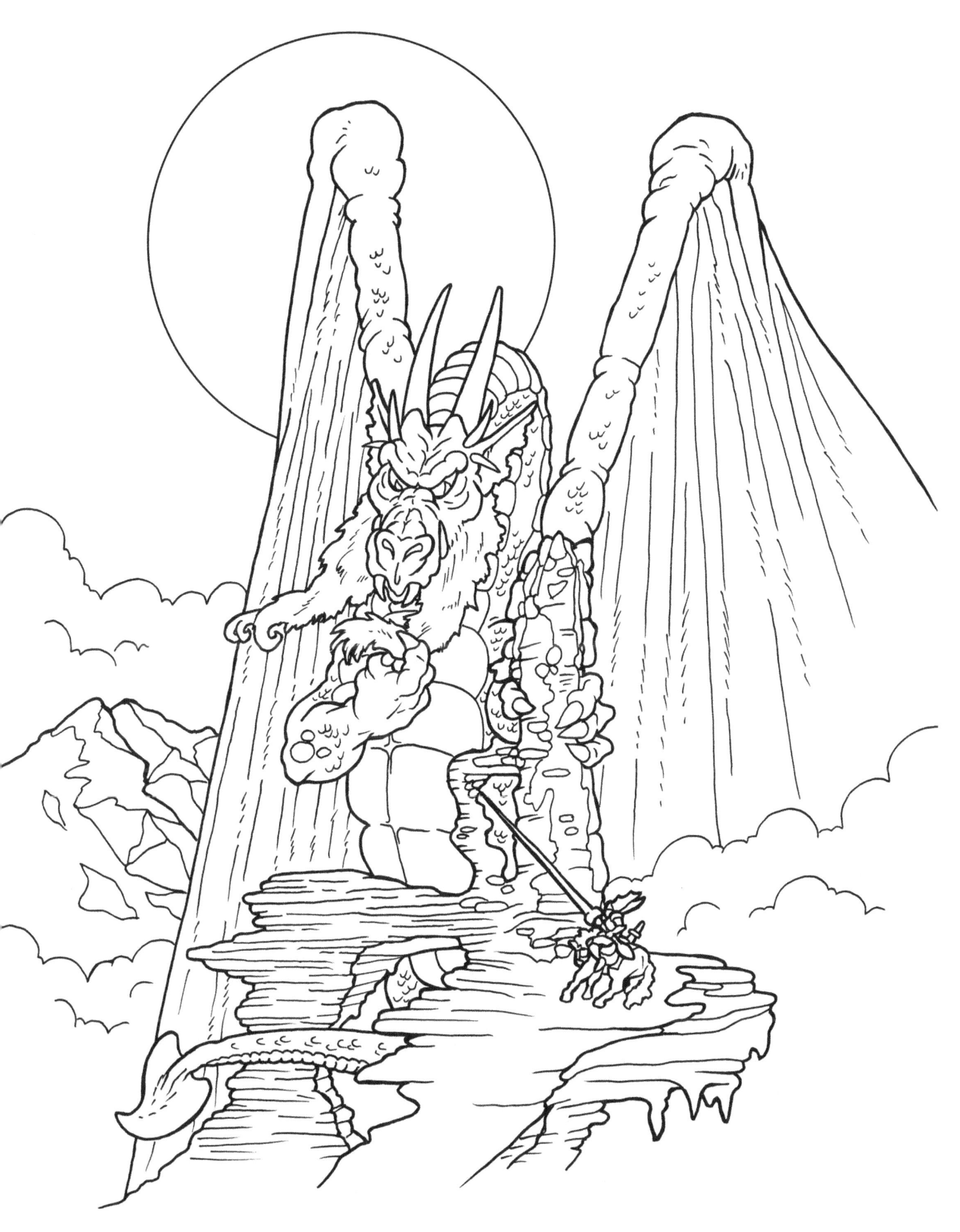

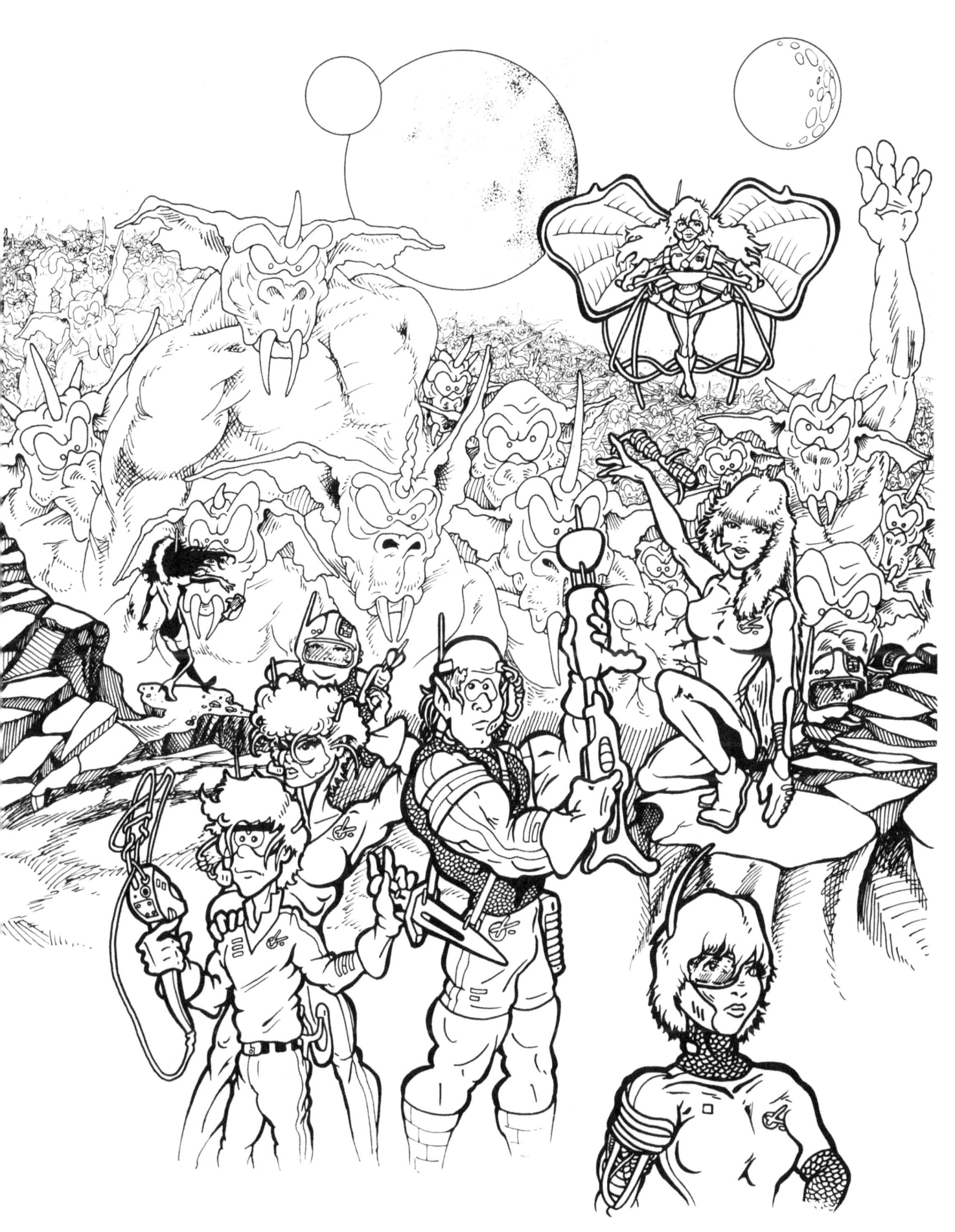

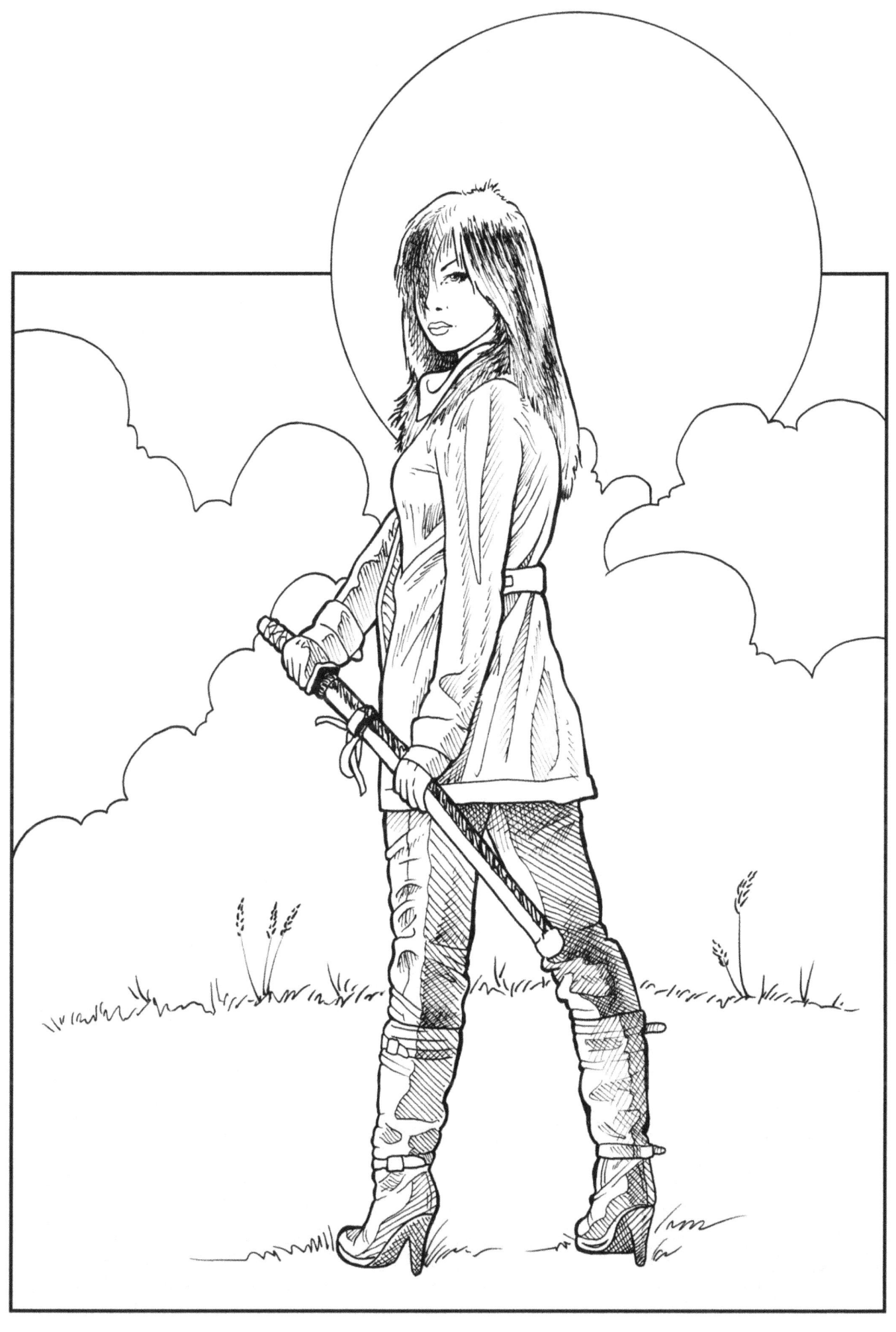

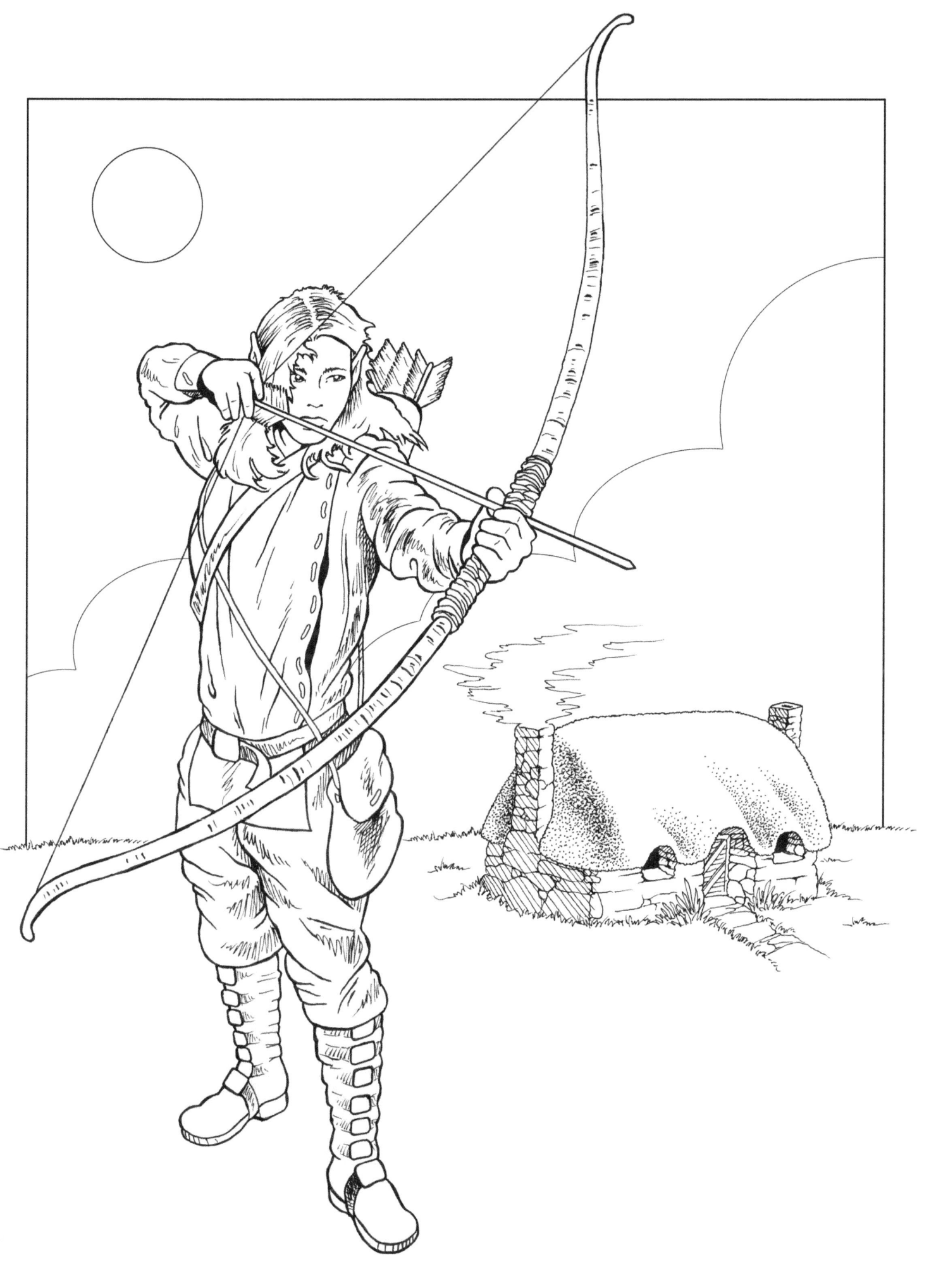

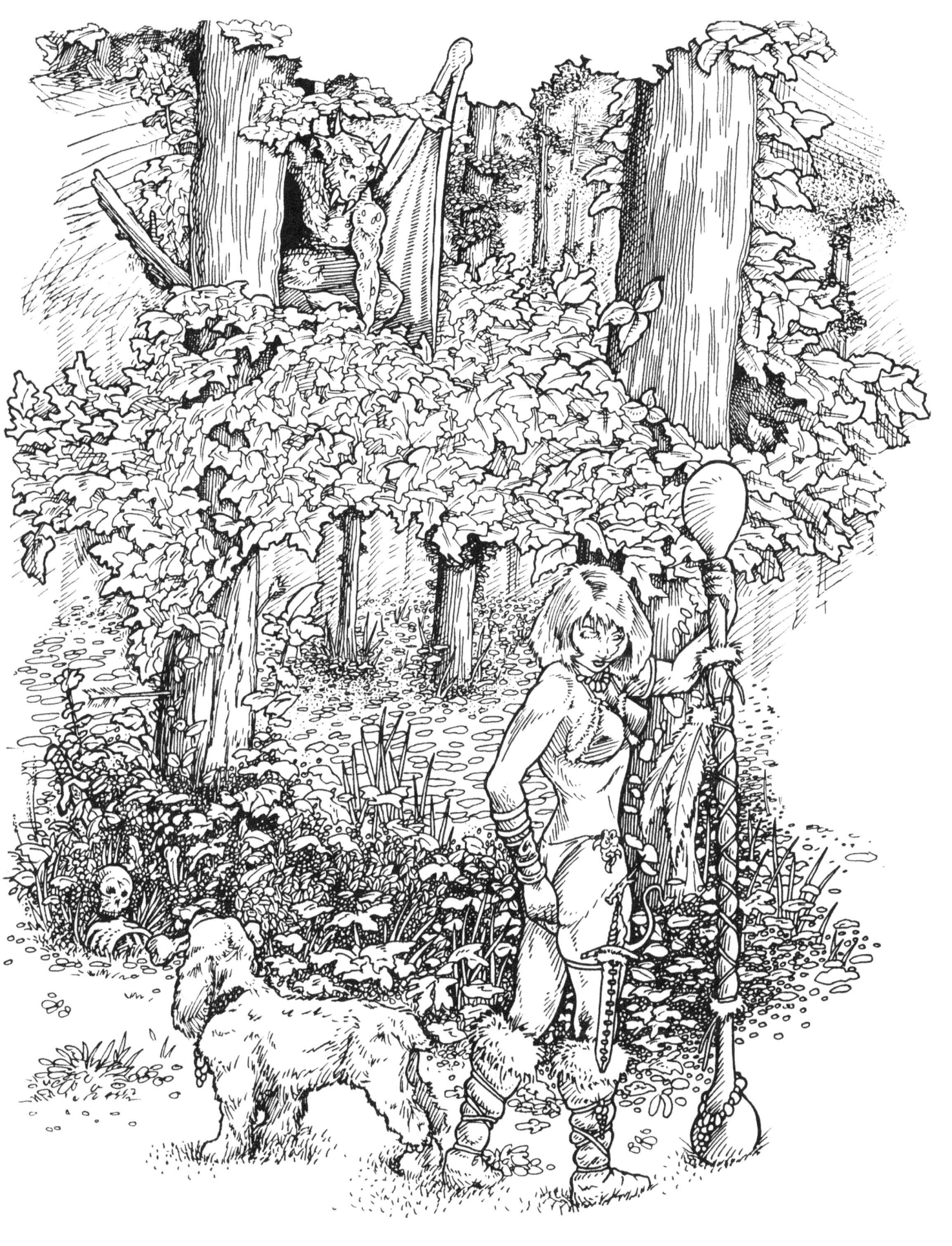

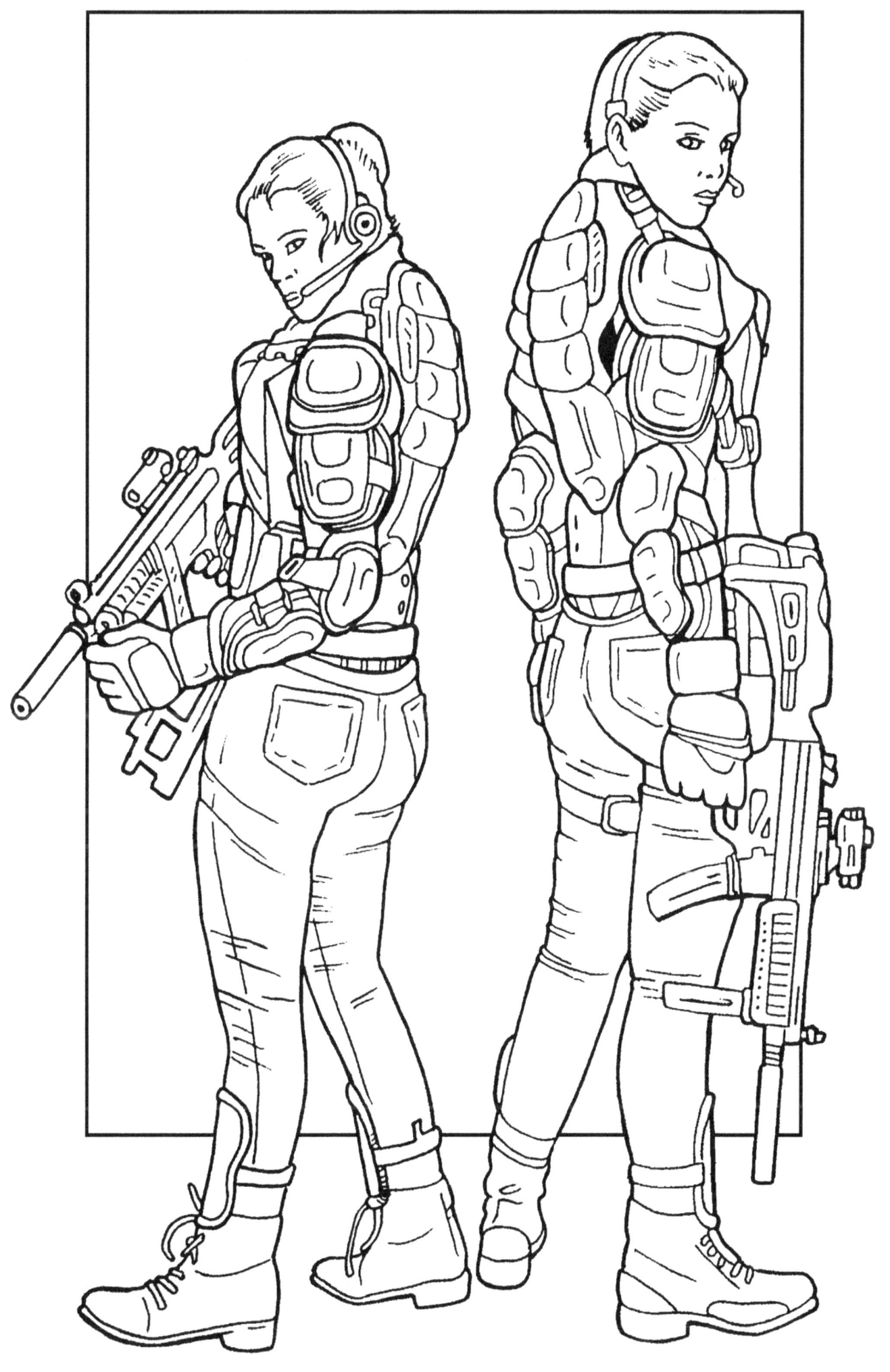

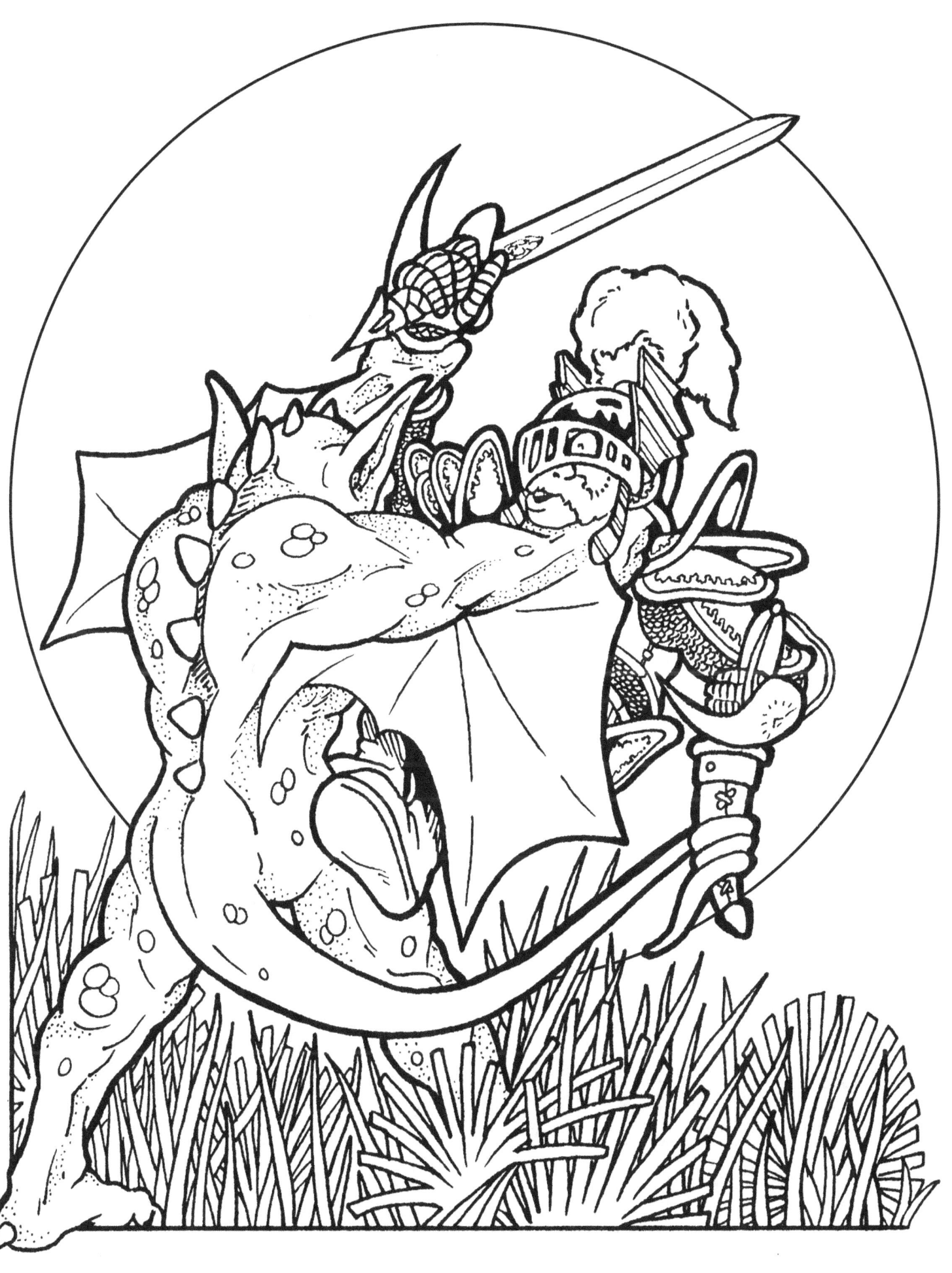

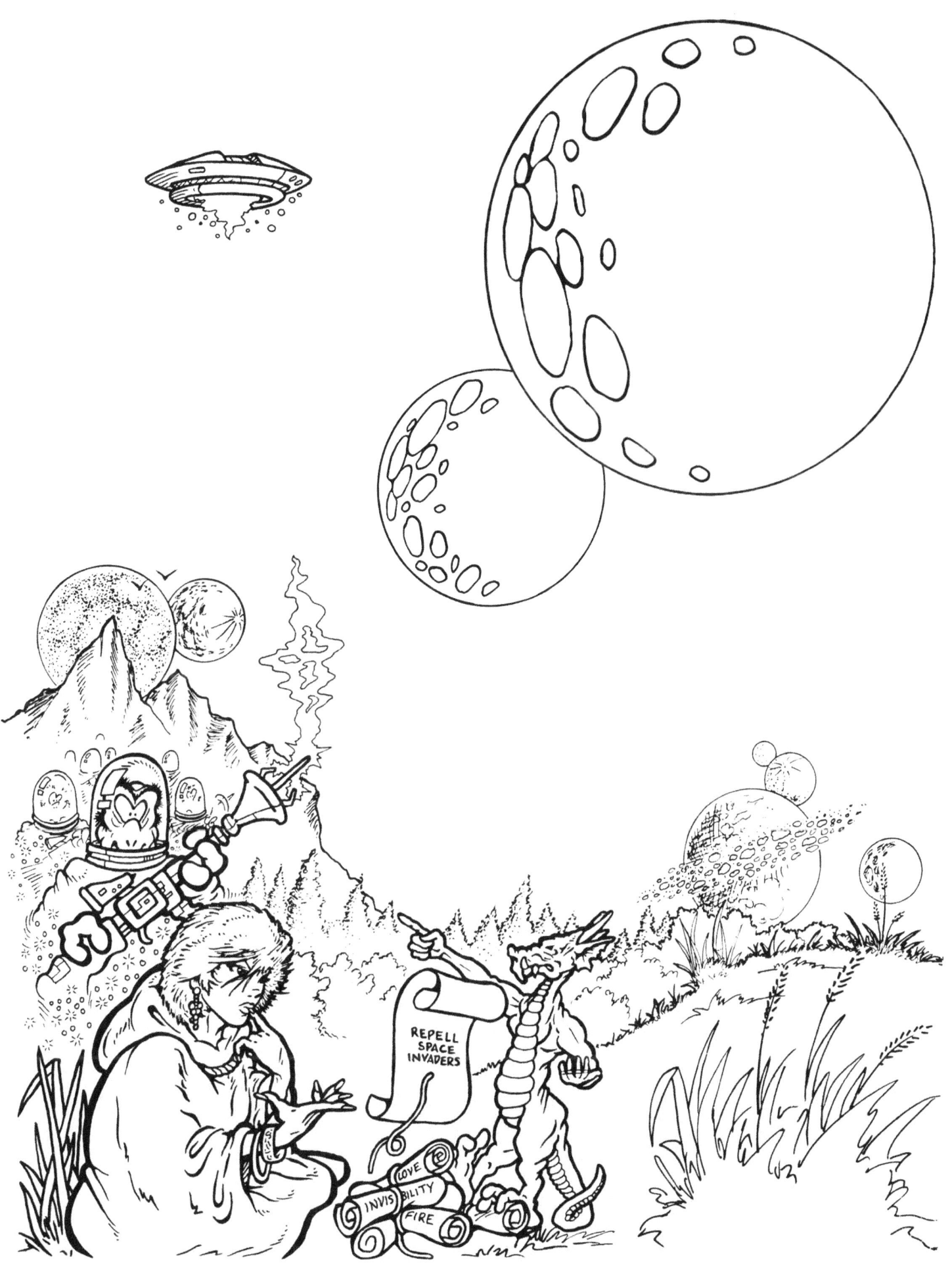

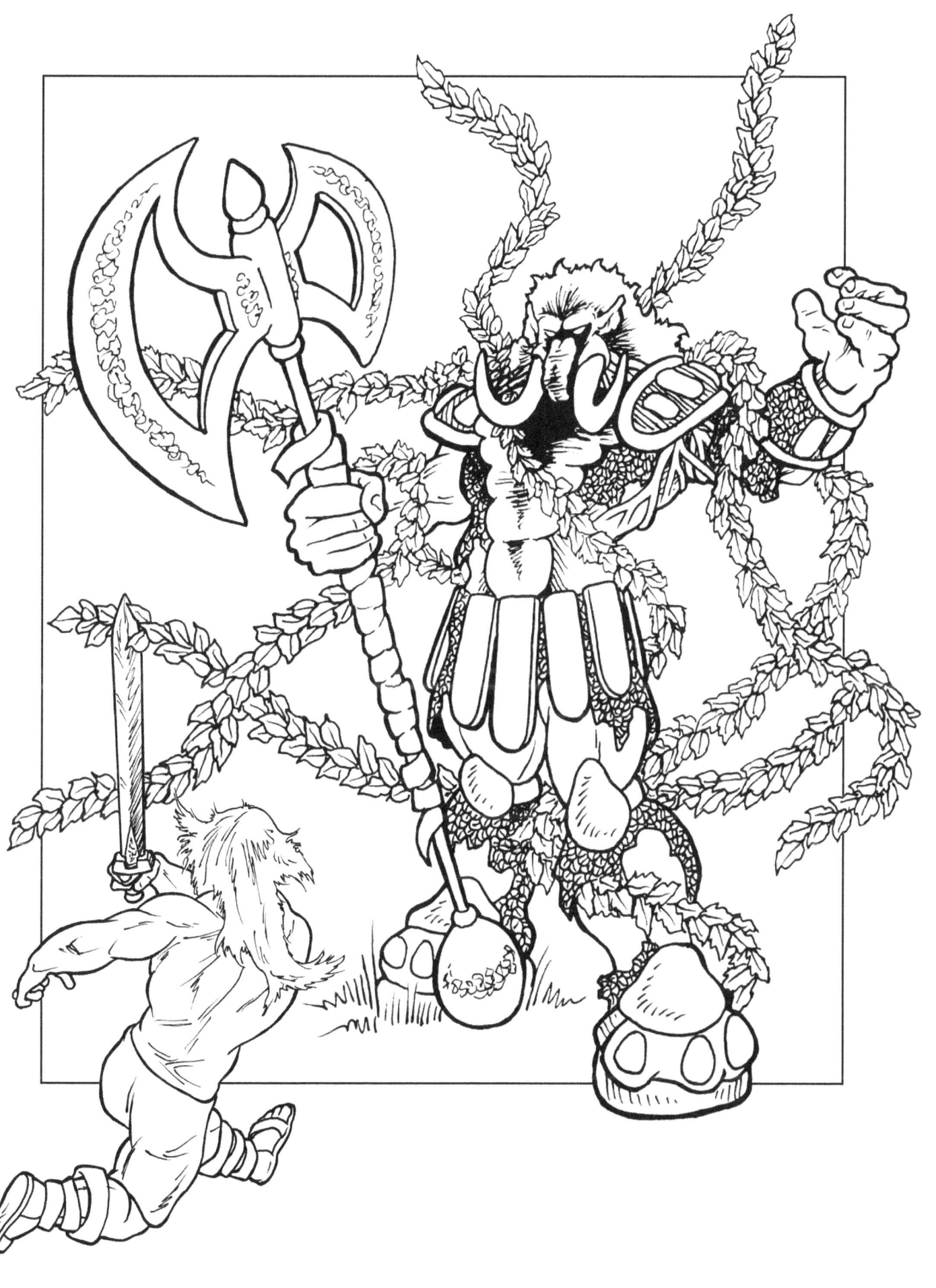

Okay—now that you've colored some pictures to begin developing your eye-hand coordination skills, let's move on to the drawing part of this workbook.

Stick to it!

I know, "stick to it" is a bad pun when getting ready to discuss drawing stick people, but I couldn't help myself.

I don't know how many times I've had someone tell me they couldn't even draw stick people. I don't believe them. The truth of the matter is most of us have doodled stick people on our pages at least once or twice in our lives. I grant you it may have been years since you've tried to draw a stick person, but like riding a bike, it's something you never forget how to do.

Let's give it a try. Use the stick people below as your guide. You'll notice they're a bit more detailed than the typical stick person—they have a line connecting the arms for shoulders and a line connecting the legs for the hips—but all-in-all they're just stick people.

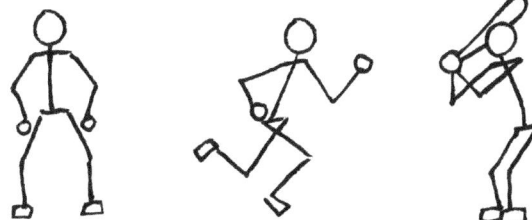

Don't worry about putting a lot of detail in the hands and feet. We're more interested in making them do things. Draw your stick people running, dancing, jumping, climbing—whatever activity you can think of. Look at pictures and photos and see if you can draw your stick person doing what they're doing. Feel free to add props and backgrounds. A square and a triangle can give you a house. A line and some squiggles can form a tree. A circle becomes a ball and an oval or rectangle becomes a bat. The details are not important—drawing the action is what you are working on.

Use a pencil. Until you get comfortable drawing with a pencil you shouldn't try using a pen or marker.

Fill the bottom of this page and the following two pages with your stick people. Make them do whatever you can come up with. You're not creating one big scene, but lots of small scenes all over the page. When you're finished with the doodle page, move onto the next step in the book. However, feel free to continue drawing stick people on a piece of paper if you're not comfortable moving on yet (I've included work pages at the back of the book). Also, as you progress through the book, continue to draw stick people when you're not working on the other drawing exercises. If you don't have this book with you or you don't have time to work on your art skills, doodling is a great way to keep your brain in draw mode.

Doodle Page

Fill these pages with your stick people doing things.

Doodle Page

Tracing

Tracing pictures is a great way to get your brain comfortable with drawing. Using a piece of tracing paper or tracing vellum and a pencil, trace the picture of the robot holding the pencil. Don't worry if your lines aren't perfect—we're just giving your hand a little practice creating lines that go together to form a picture. This is your first step in learning to control your pencil.

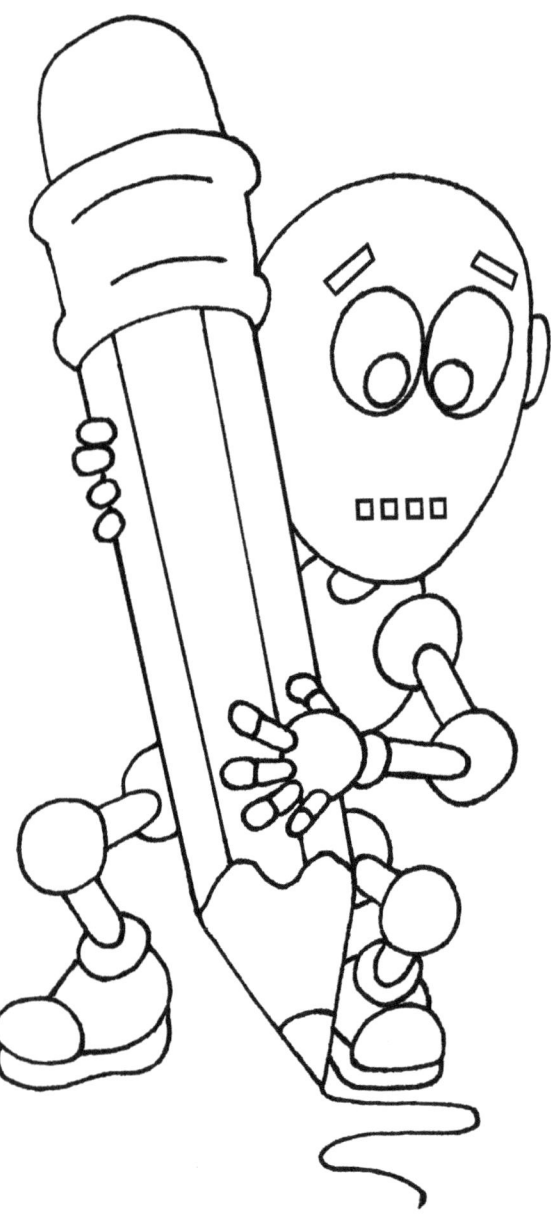

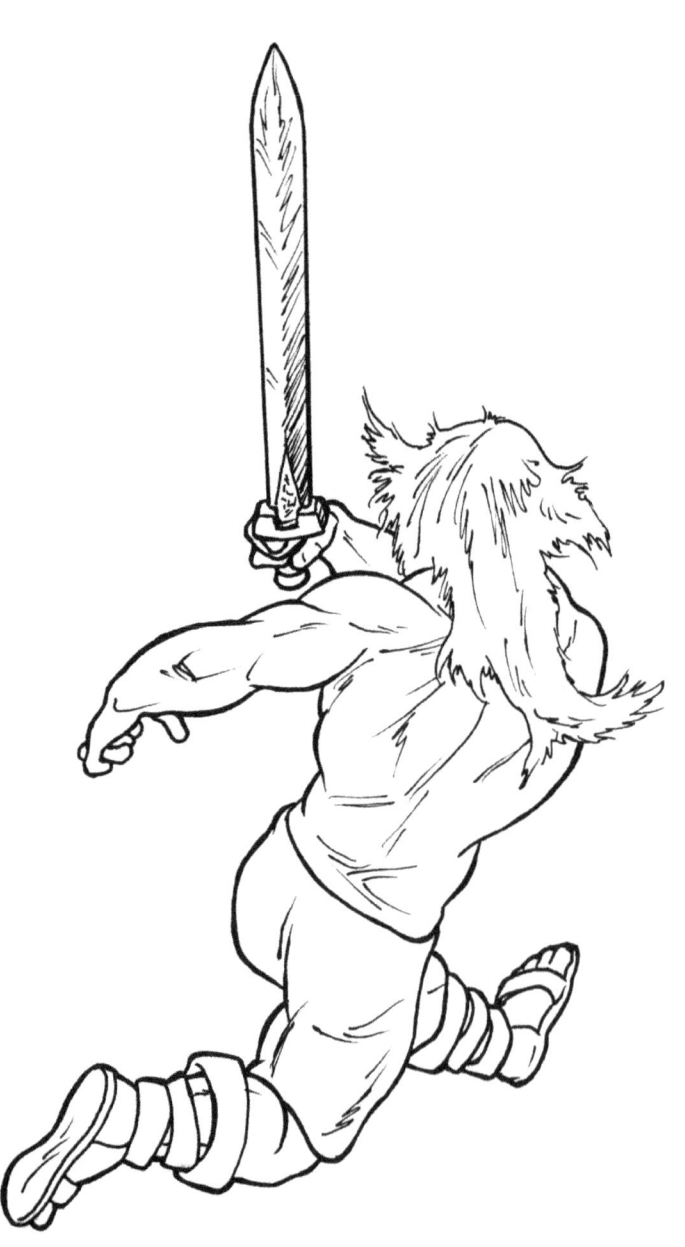

Now trace the running barbarian to the right. I've purposely given you a picture that includes different line thicknesses and minor shading. Don't worry about trying to copy the thickness of the lines or the shading, just pay attention to where and how they're used. In some cases you will be forced to figure out where the line is due to the shading or line thickness.

Here are a few more pictures for you to trace. These are a little more complicated than the first two, but if you take your time they shouldn't be too difficult to trace.

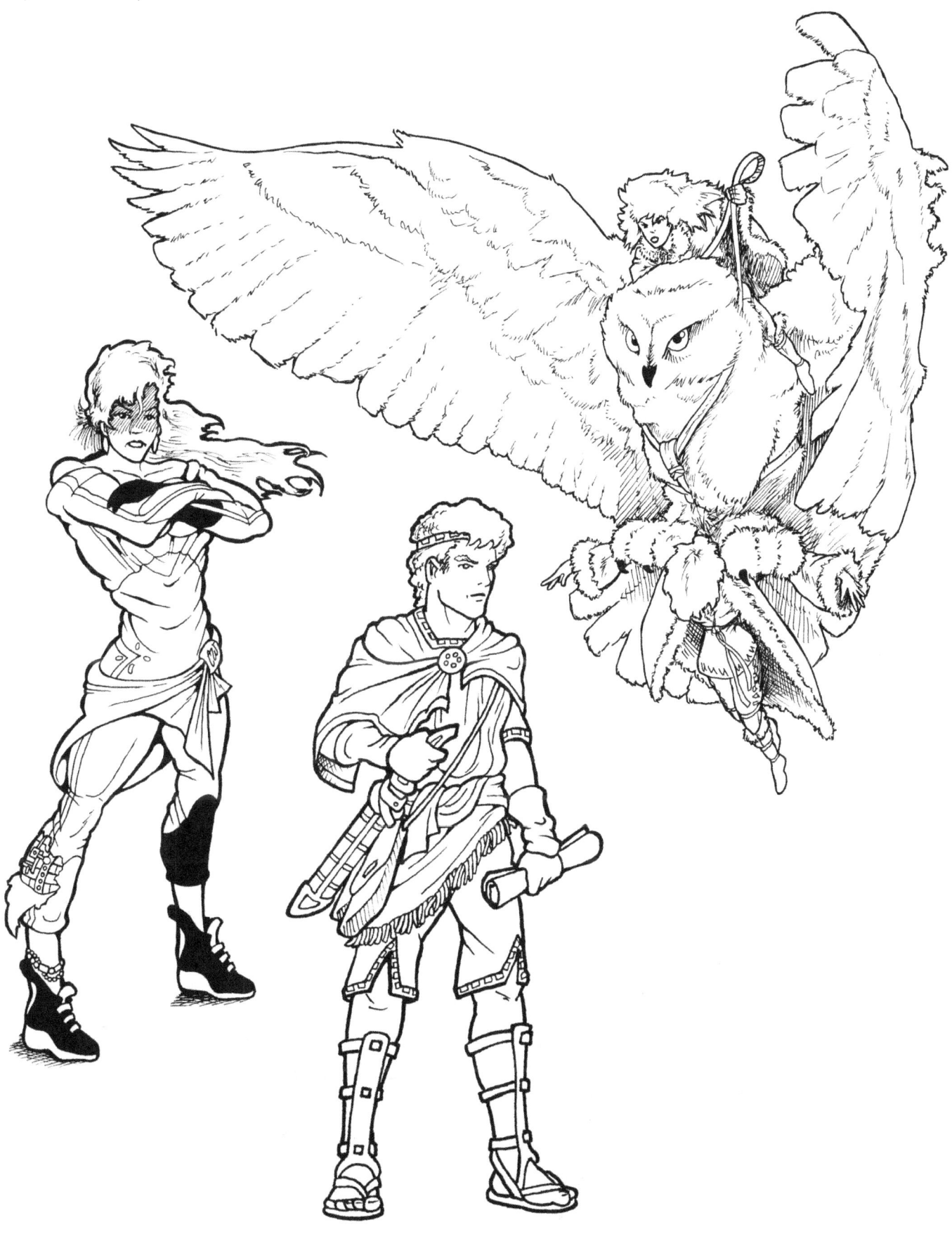

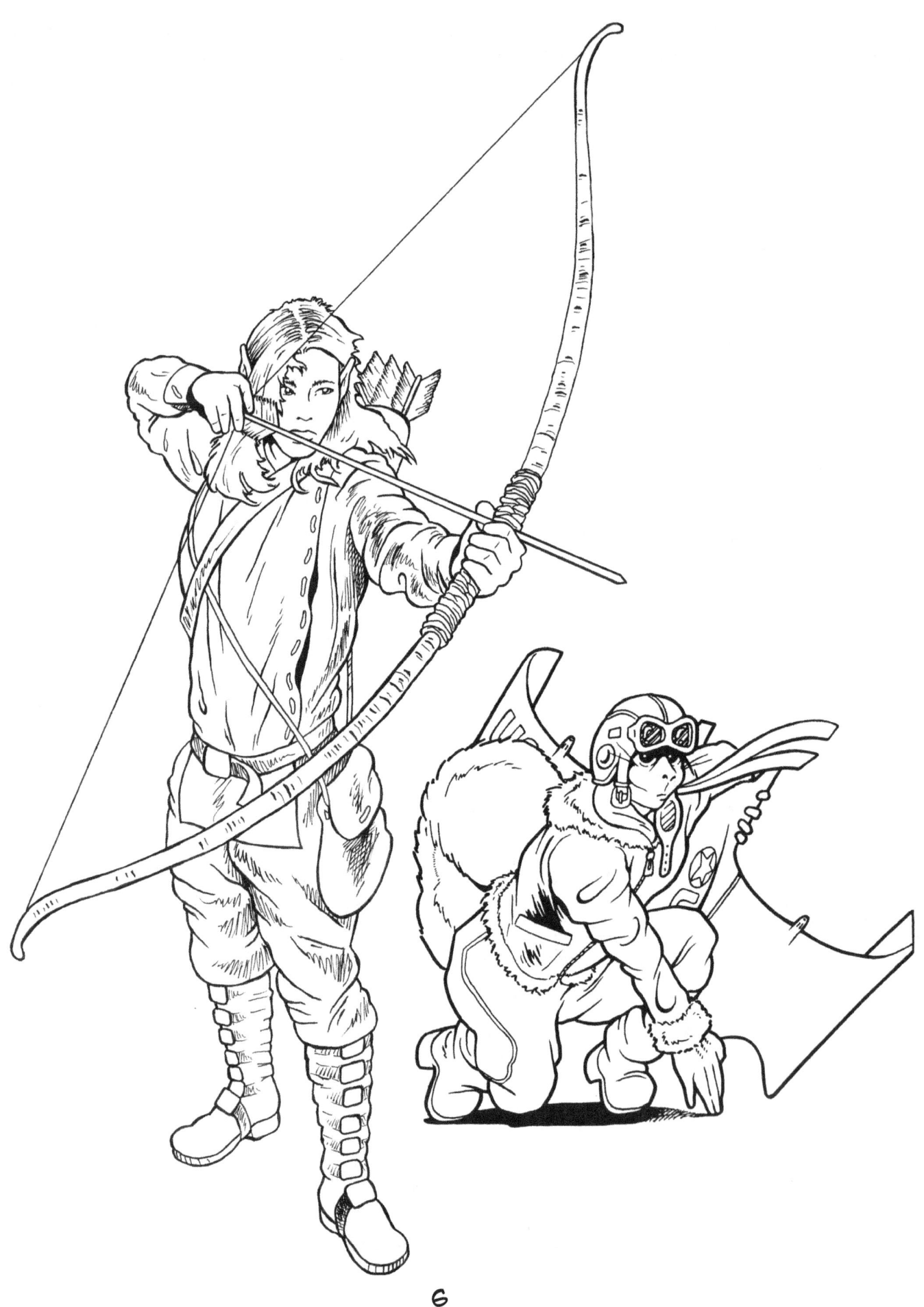

Try tracing the picture below. I've given you this picture because it has a lot of shading and variation in lines, but otherwise it's a fairly simple picture. See if you can trace the picture without drawing any of the shading. When you're done with this, go through this book and try your hand at tracing some of the coloring book pictures. Once you're happy with the quality of the pictures you're creating by tracing, move on to the next section in the book.

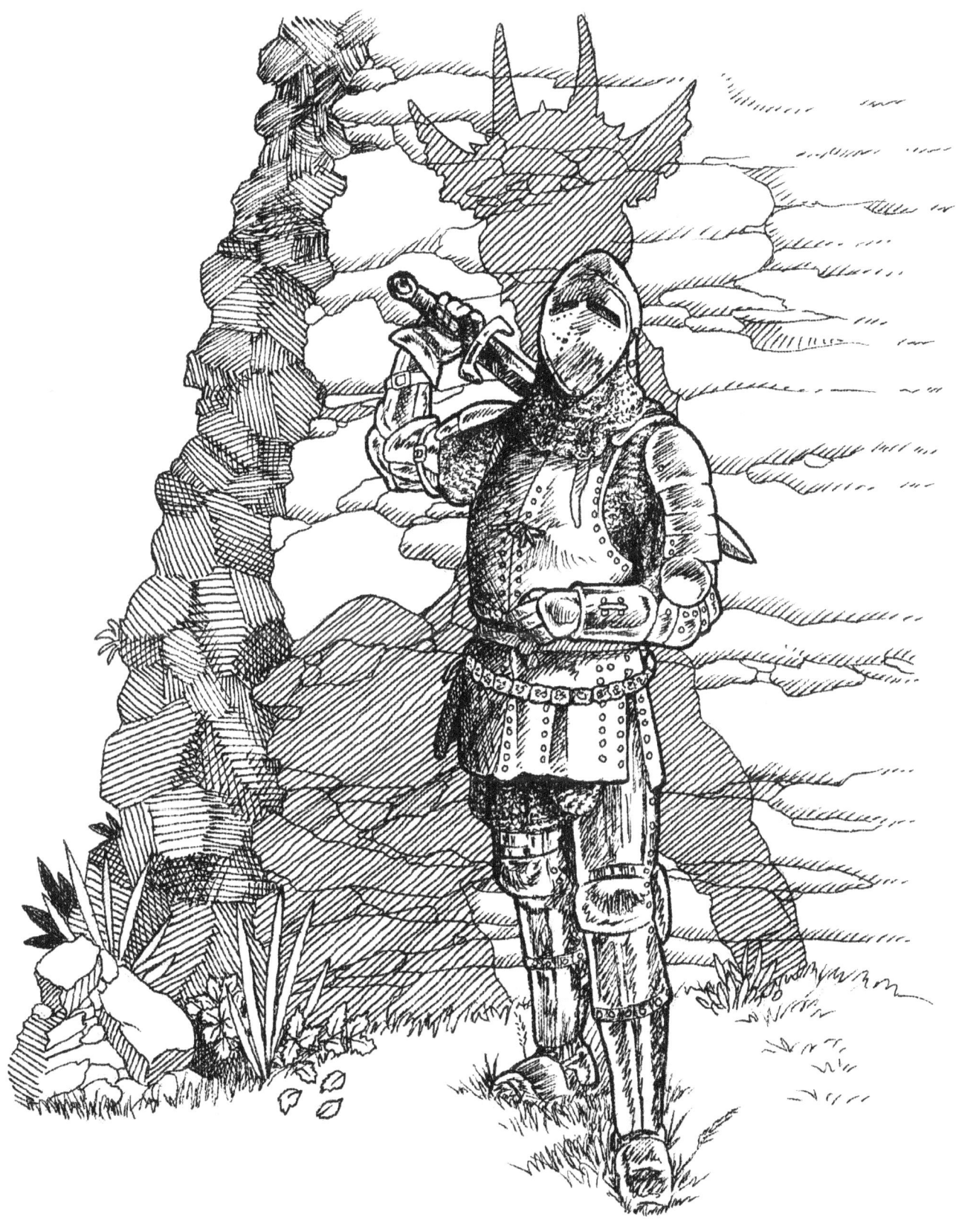

Grids

Grids are a great way to break a picture down into smaller parts to make copying a picture easier. We've all played games where you use the numbers or letters across the top and side of a grid to locate your target or place your playing pieces. Well, this is a lot like that.

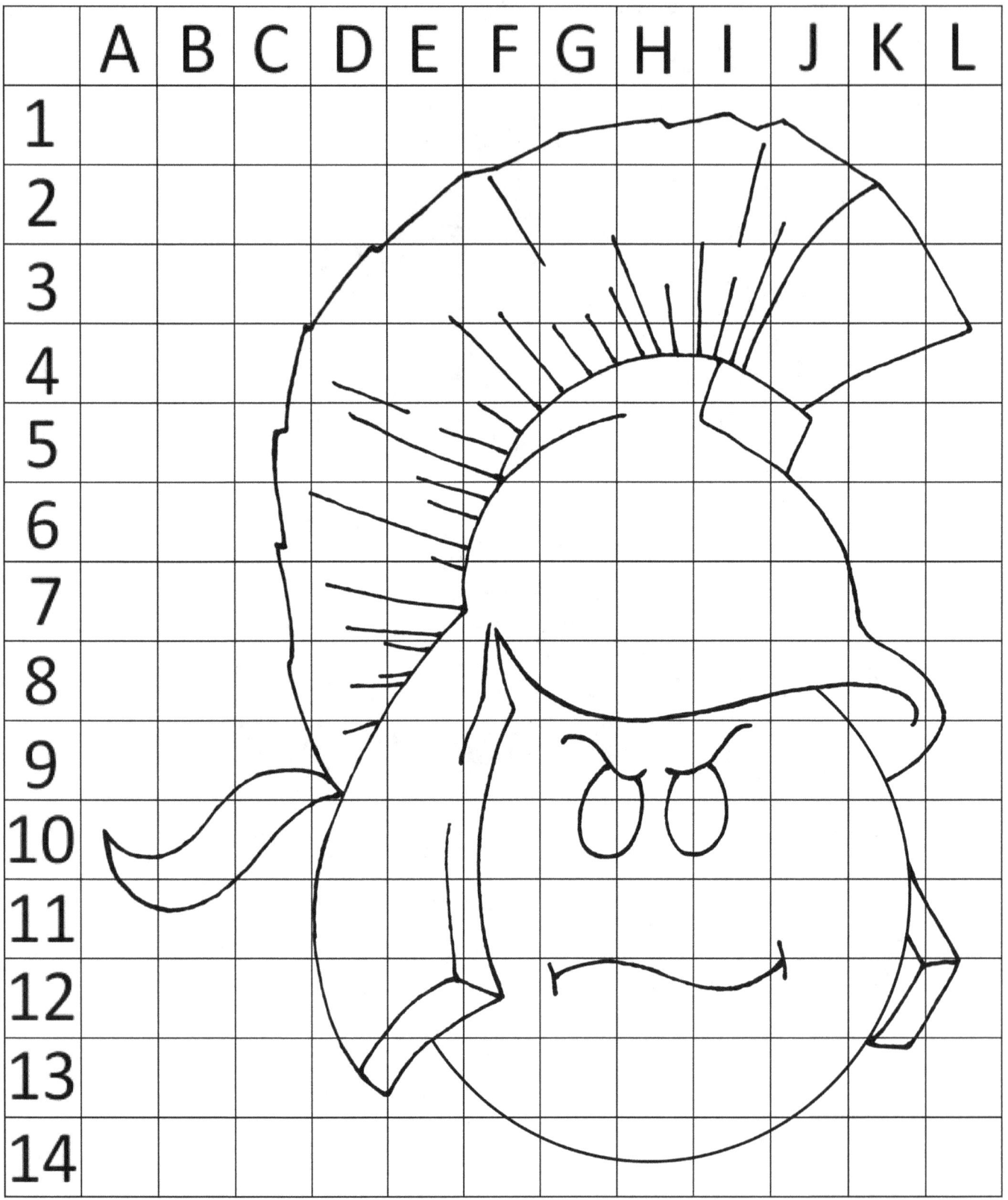

Use the grid on the left page as your guide to copy the picture to the grid below. I've given you some of the picture to get you started.

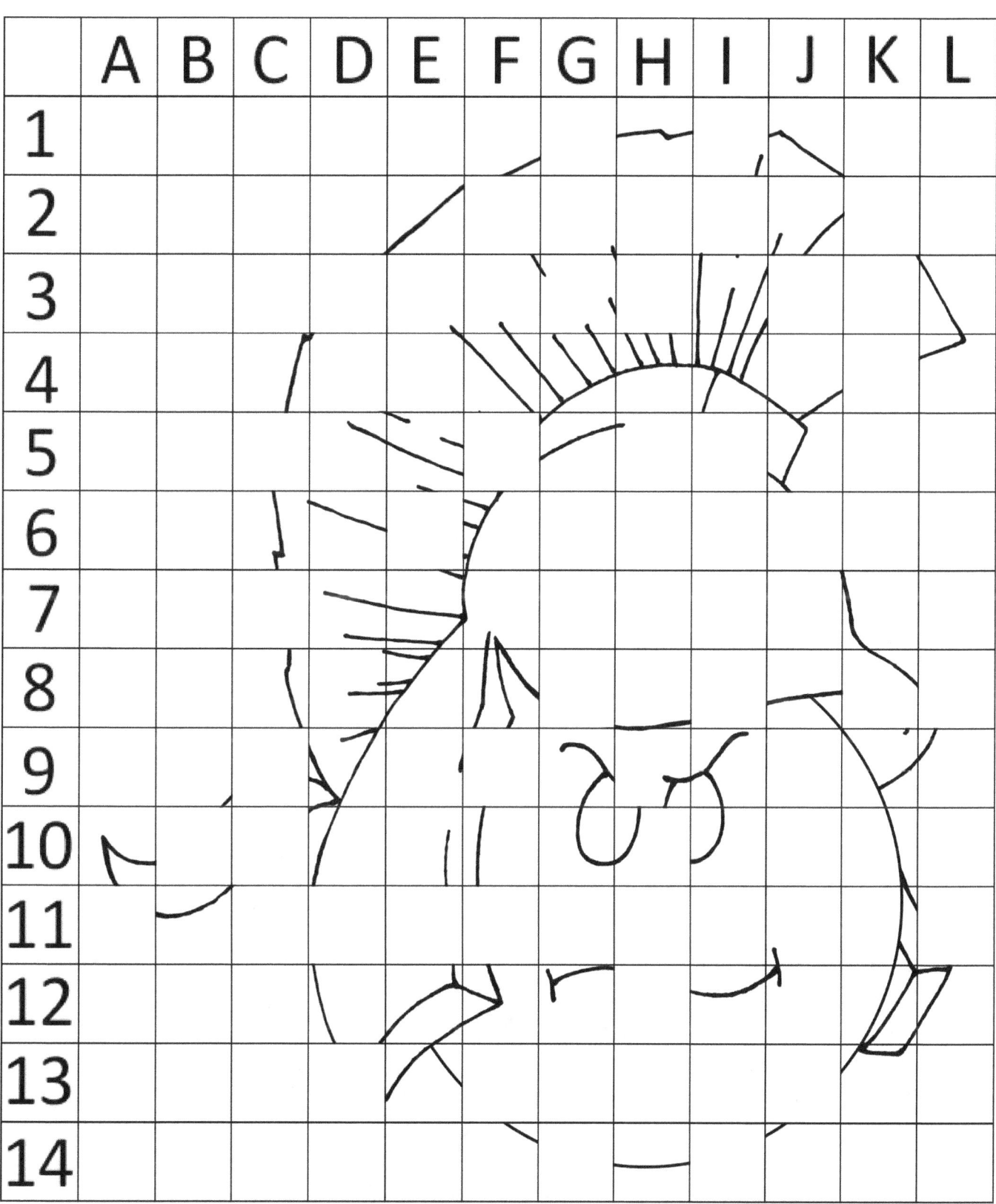

9

Here's another one. Copy from the left grid to the right grid just as you did with the previous picture.

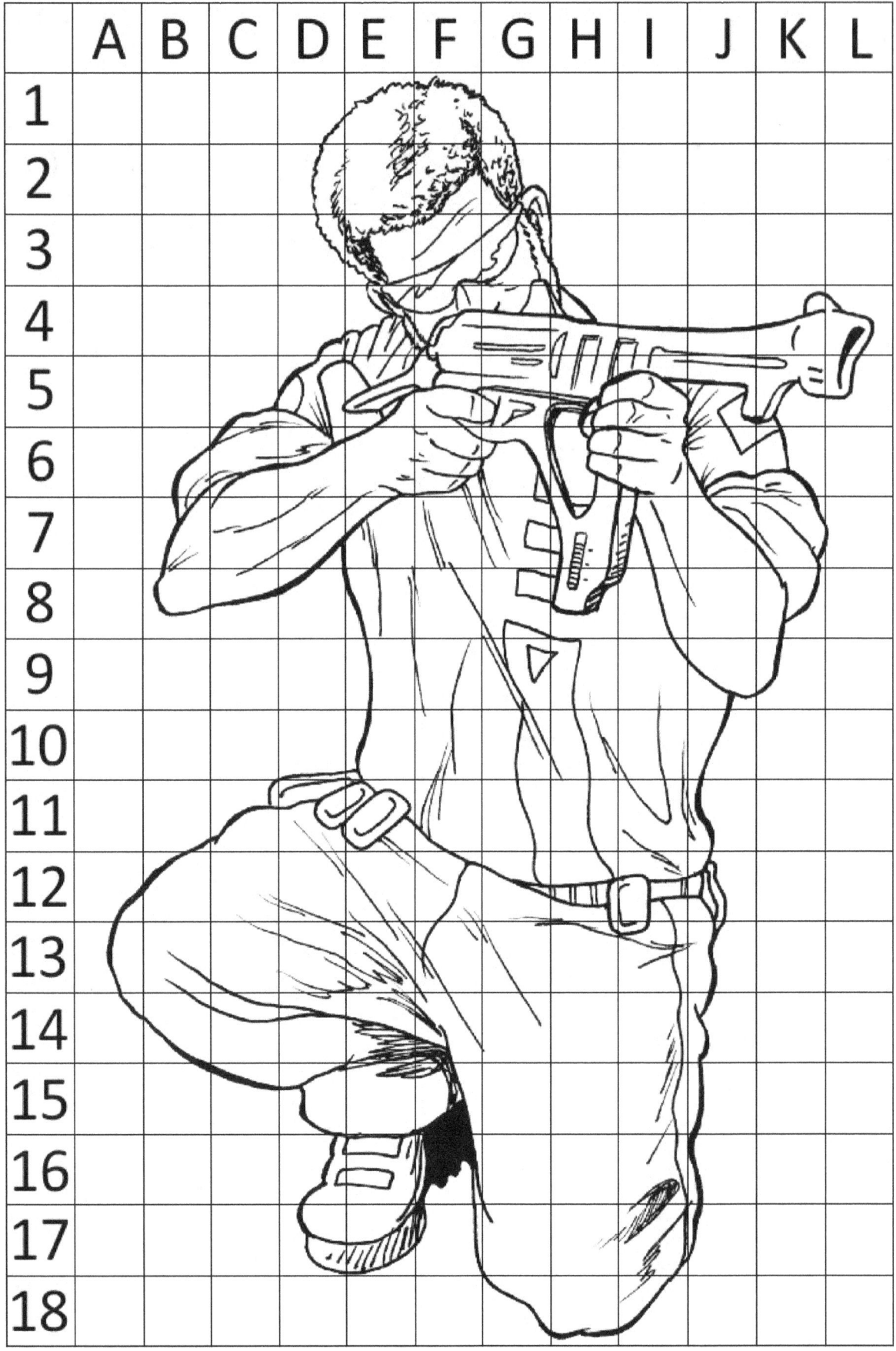

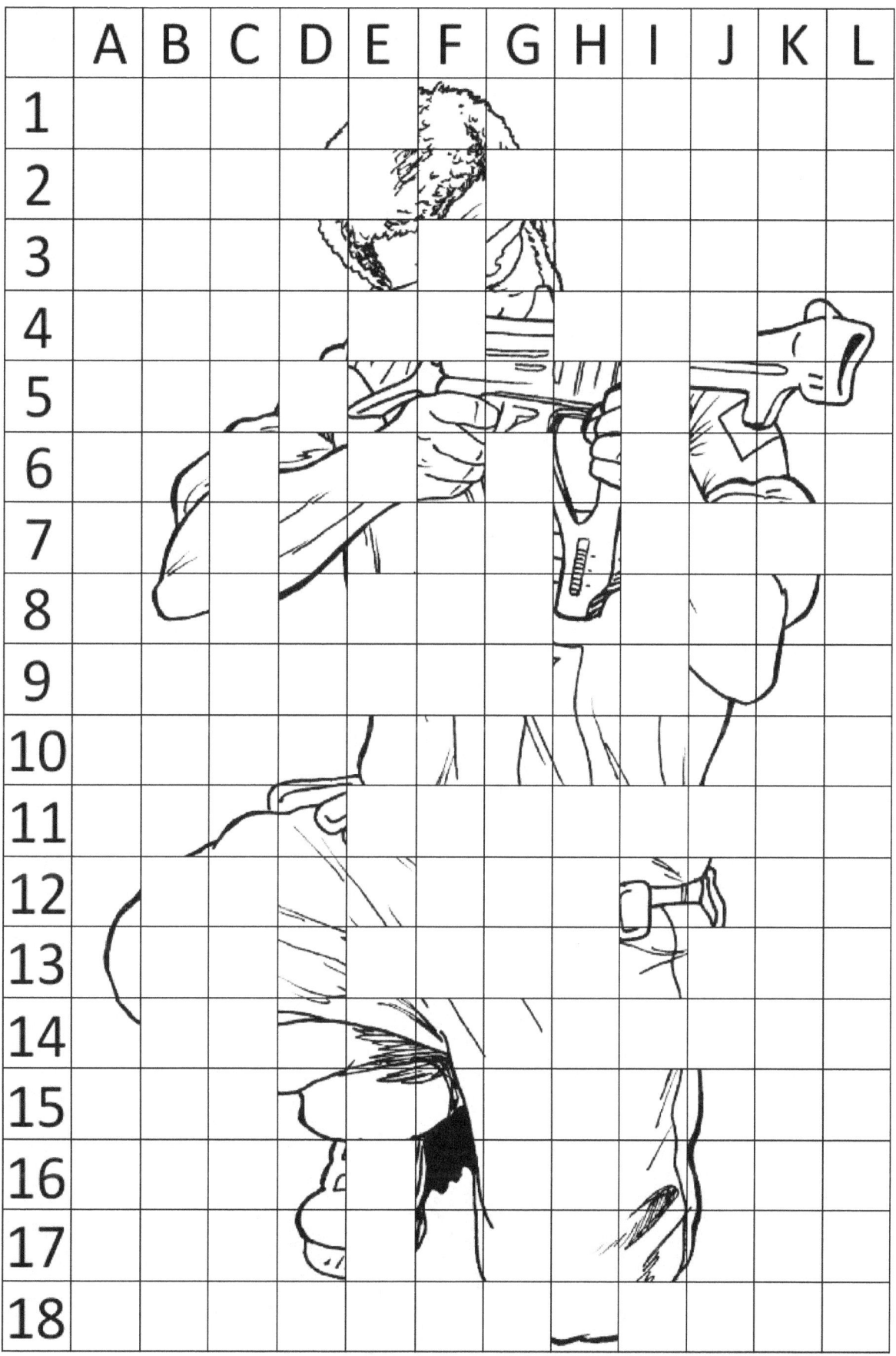

Now try your hand at copying this picture to the empty grid. Don't worry about the lines used for shading. You can copy them or ignore them. Then work the next few pages.

| | A | B | C | D | E | F | G | H | I | J | K |

1
2
3
4
5
6
7
8
9
10
11
12
13
14
15
16
17
18

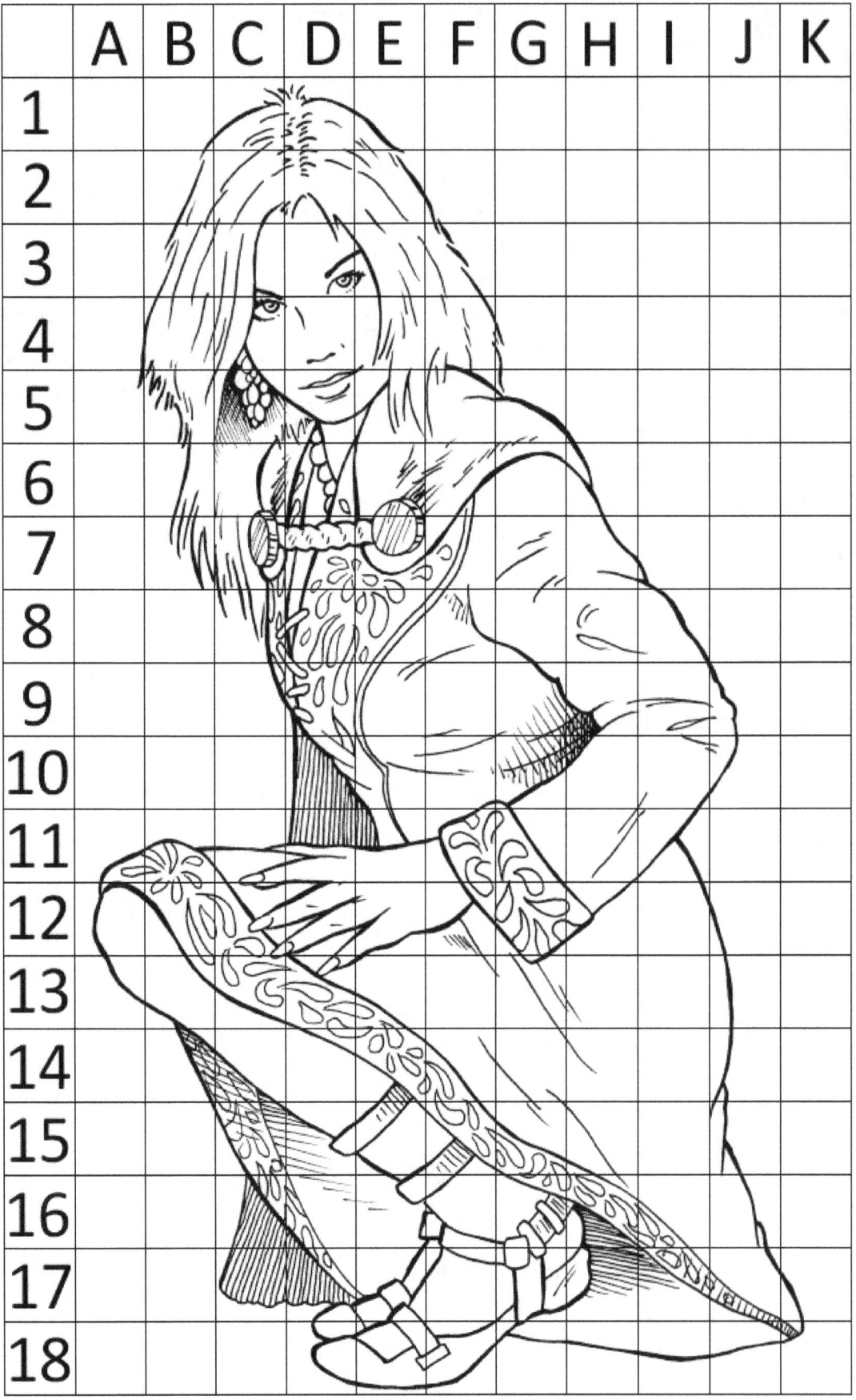

	A	B	C	D	E	F	G	H	I	J	K
1											
2											
3											
4											
5											
6											
7											
8											
9											
10											
11											
12											
13											
14											
15											
16											
17											
18											

	A	B	C	D	E	F	G	H
1								
2								
3								
4								
5								
6								
7								
8								
9								
10								
11								
12								
13								
14								
15								
16								
17								
18								

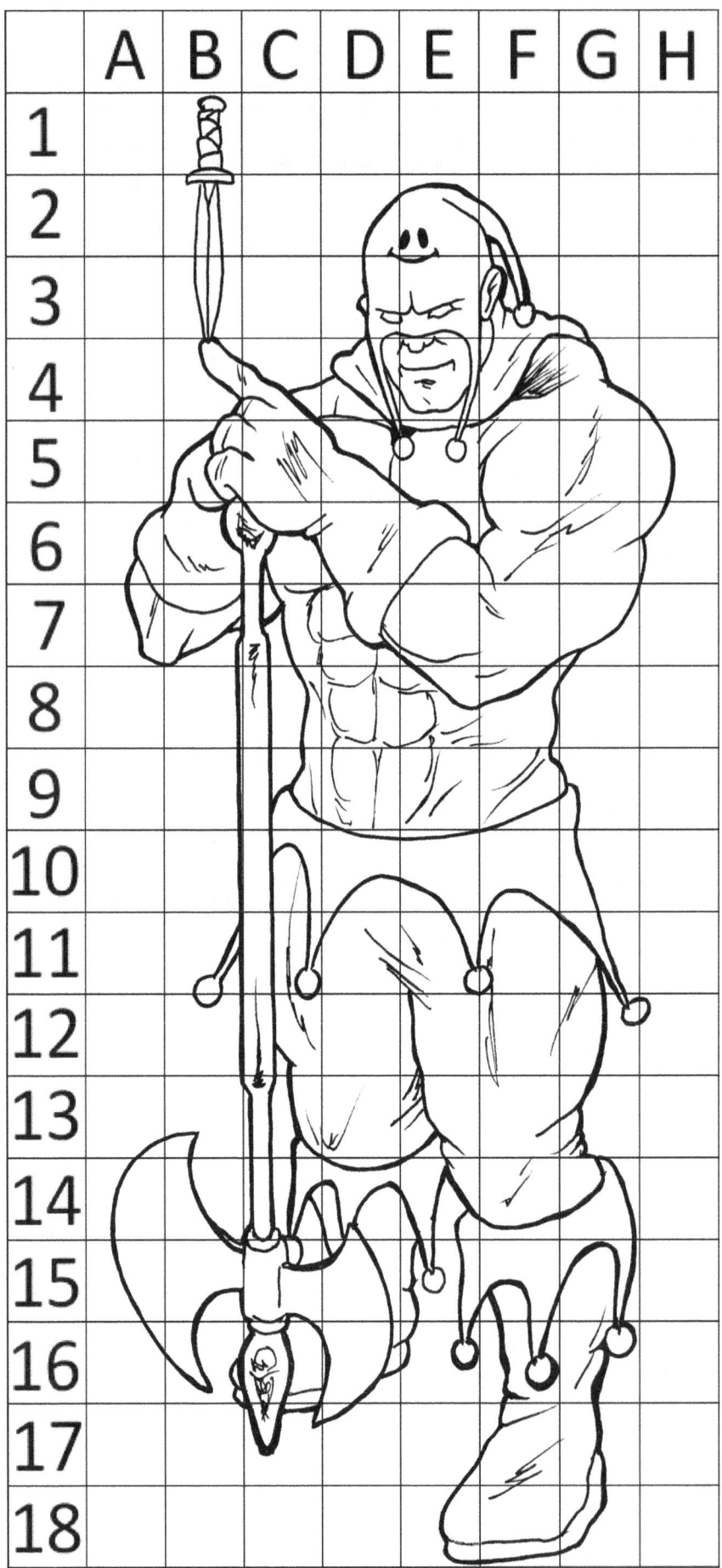

14

	A	B	C	D	E	F	G	H
1								
2								
3								
4								
5								
6								
7								
8								
9								
10								
11								
12								
13								
14								
15								
16								
17								
18								

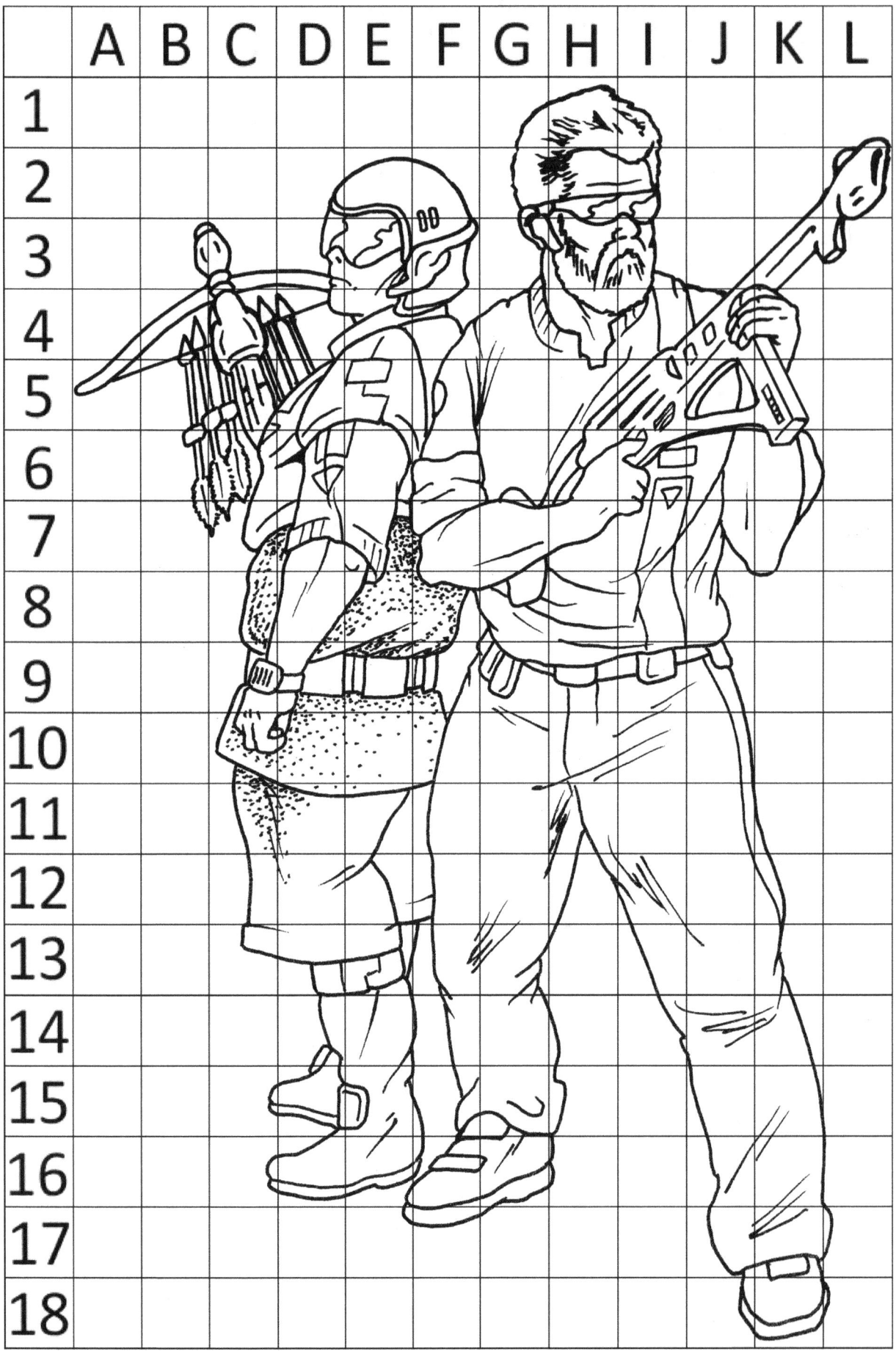

	A	B	C	D	E	F	G	H	I	J	K	L
1												
2												
3												
4												
5												
6												
7												
8												
9												
10												
11												
12												
13												
14												
15												
16												
17												
18												

	A	B	C	D	E	F	G	H	I	J	K	L
1												
2												
3												
4												
5												
6												
7												
8												
9												
10												
11												

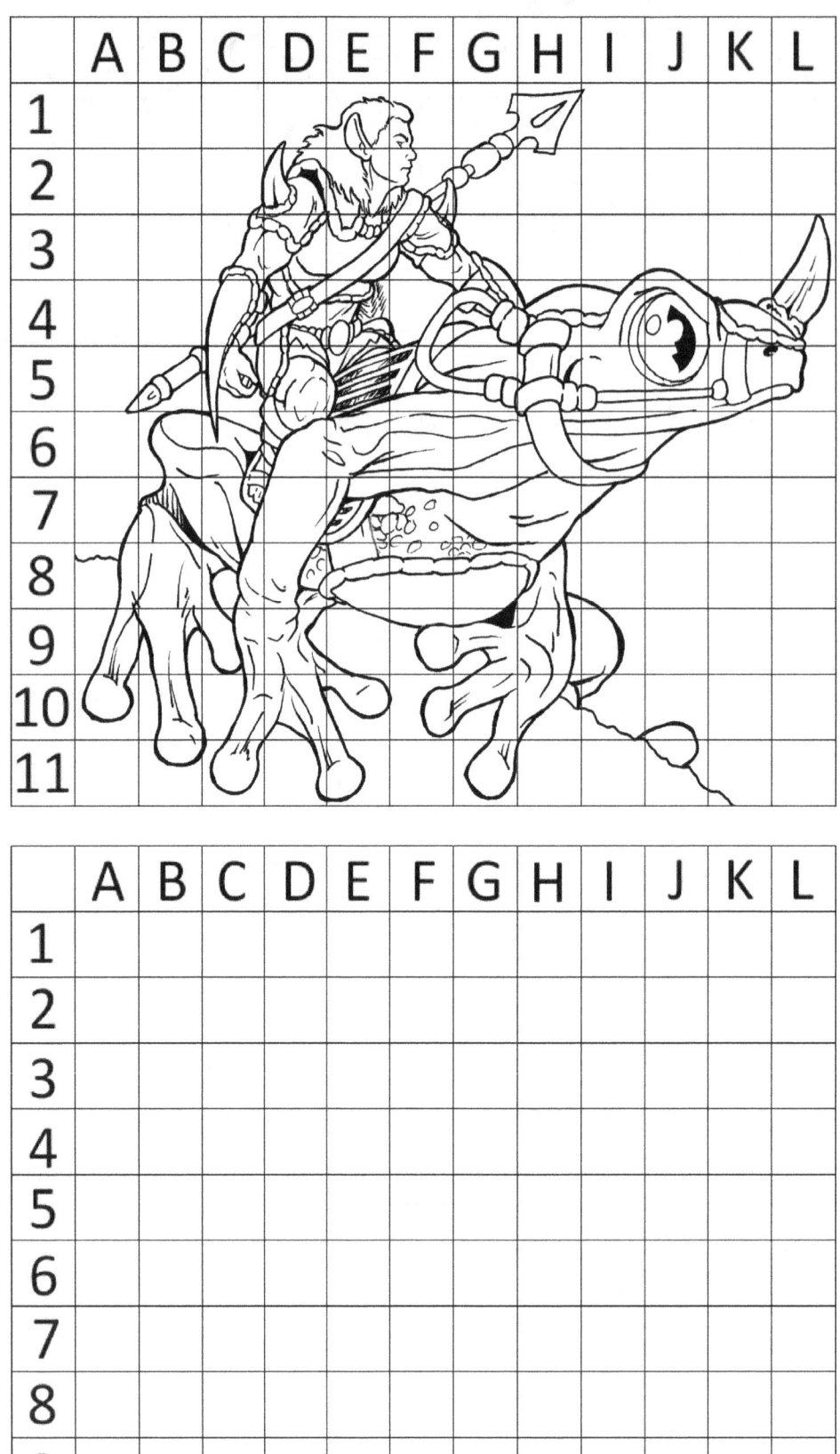

	A	B	C	D	E	F	G	H	I	J	K	L
1												
2												
3												
4												
5												
6												
7												
8												
9												
10												
11												

	A	B	C	D	E	F	G	H	I	J	K	L
1												
2												
3												
4												
5												
6												
7												
8												
9												
10												

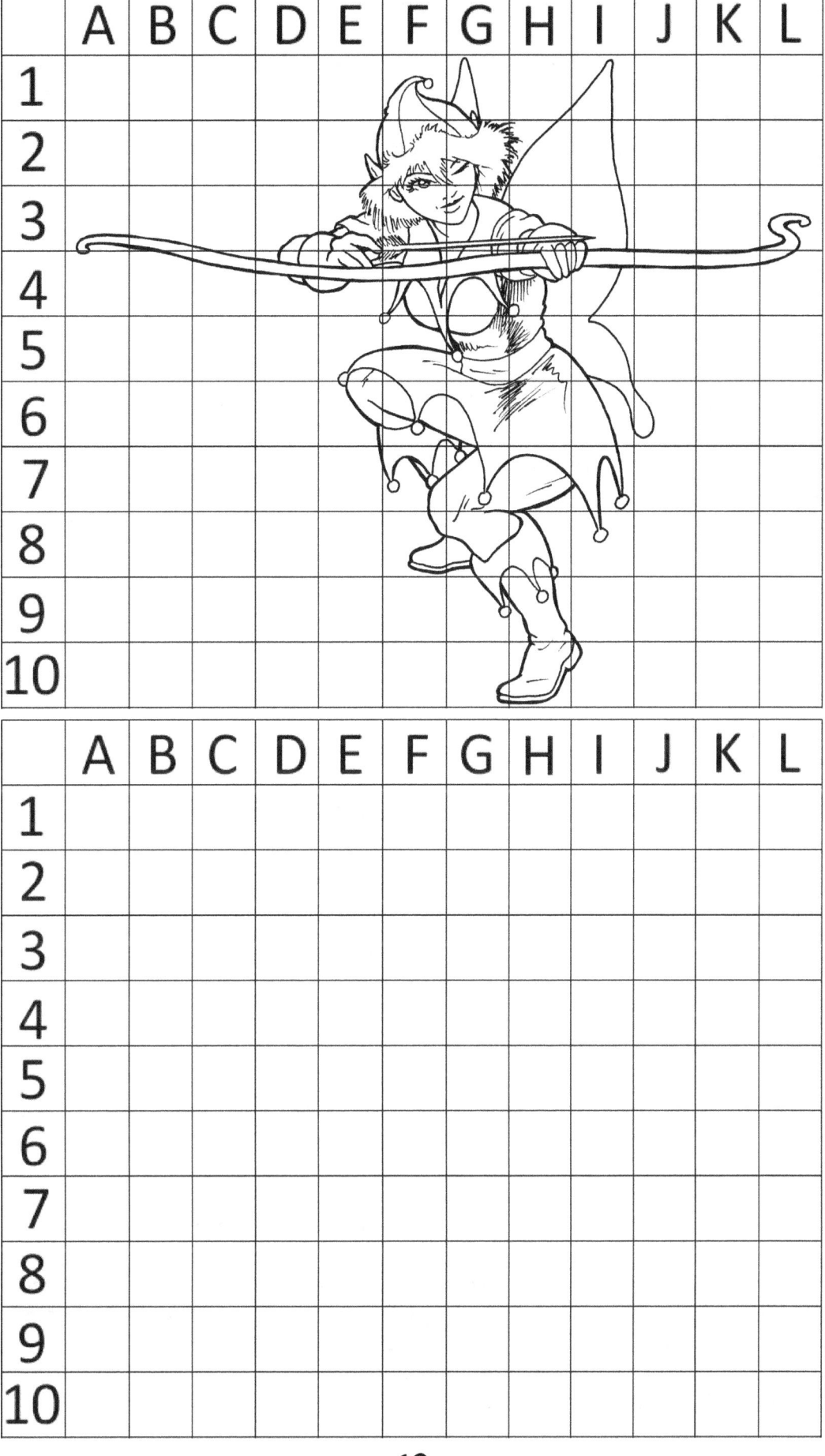

	A	B	C	D	E	F	G	H	I	J	K	L
1												
2												
3												
4												
5												
6												
7												
8												
9												
10												

If you feel that you still need to do a few more grids before moving on, use a straightedge (ruler) to trace one of the grids in this book to a page of tracing paper (or vellum). Either make a copy of one of the coloring pages in this book (before you color it) or tear the page out. OR just find a simple line drawing in another coloring book. Place the vellum grid sheet over the coloring page book and—using one of the grids in the work section of this book—copy the picture to the grid (you can just focus on a part of the picture if you don't want to copy the entire thing). You may wish to make a copy of a blank grid before you use them all up so you can have a template for future use. Continue to copy pictures to grids as often as you like until you are happy with the pictures you are copying. Don't be too concerned about perfection. Just be sure you are doing a good job of finding and copying the main lines in the picture.

Once you are done, it's time to move onto using shape grids in place of line grids.

Shape Grids

You can work with shapes to create grids much the same way you used lined grids. The concept is exactly the same—it only looks different.

If you use your imagination you can find shapes (circles, ovals, triangles, rectangles, etc.) in most any picture. By overlaying those shapes onto a picture they can guide you the same way the squares in the grid did—making it easier to get proportions and details more accurately. Once you have your shapes in place, simply focus on the picture in or around each shape—drawing only those lines and moving onto the next shape when you finish (just as you did each square of the grid).

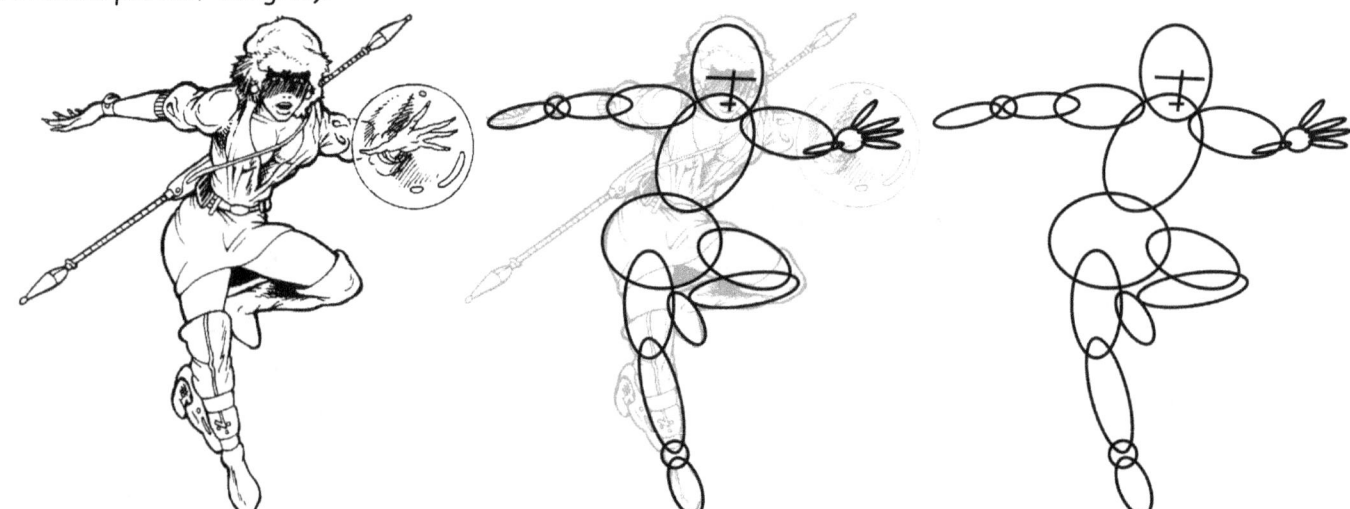

This way of copying a picture requires a little more skill than using grids, but it can be done quicker and easier than having to measure out and draw a grid.

See if this method works for you.

Use the shapes on the following pages to help you copy the picture. Remember to use the shapes just as you did the squares in the grid. They're simply there to help you break the image into smaller pieces so copying is more manageable.

When you're on your own, try the method on other pictures.

Get two pieces of tracing paper. Place one of the sheets over a drawing and put the shapes where you see them.

Using the second tracing sheet, trace the shapes you just created. Put the second sheet over a blank white piece of paper (to make it easier to work with the tracing paper) and see if you can copy the picture. After you have done this successfully a few times, try it with only one sheet of tracing paper.

Place your tracing paper over the picture and put your images where you see them. Then copy the shapes as accurately as you can (lightly) to a blank sheet of paper. Use the shapes to copy the picture.

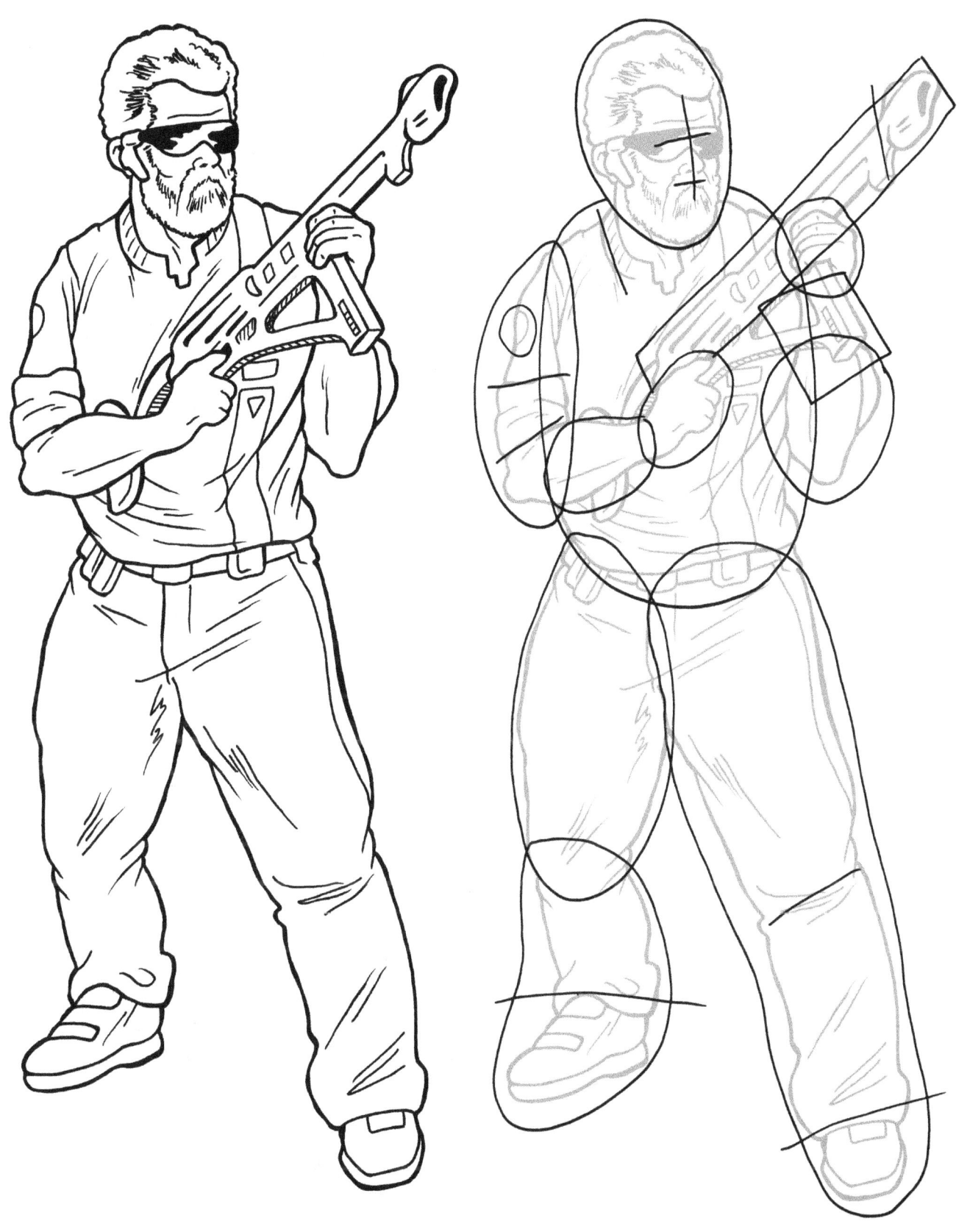

See how shapes have been drawn over parts of the body? Use the shapes as a reference so you only have to copy a small part of the picture at a time. Check out the next two pages to see if this technique works for you.

21

Here's the original picture. Use the shapes over the grayed-out image on the next page as a reference to copy the picture into the other set of shapes. I've given you a few parts of the picture to get you started.

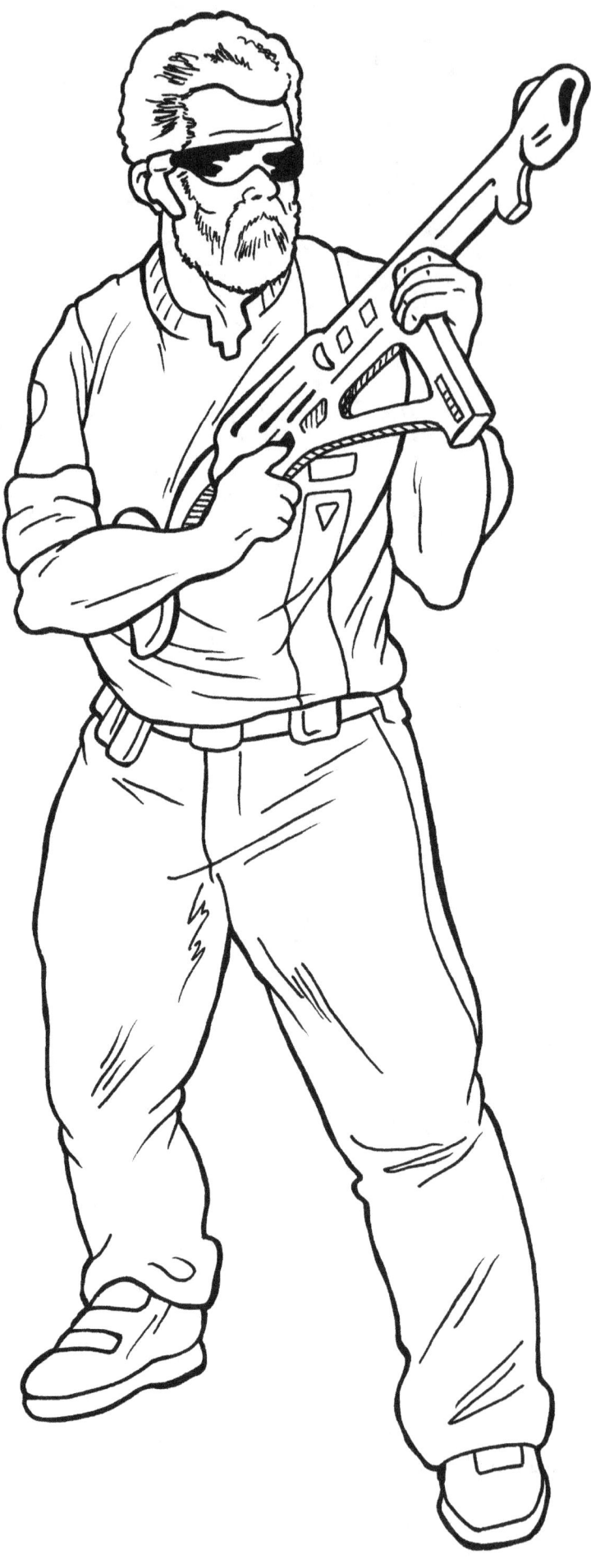

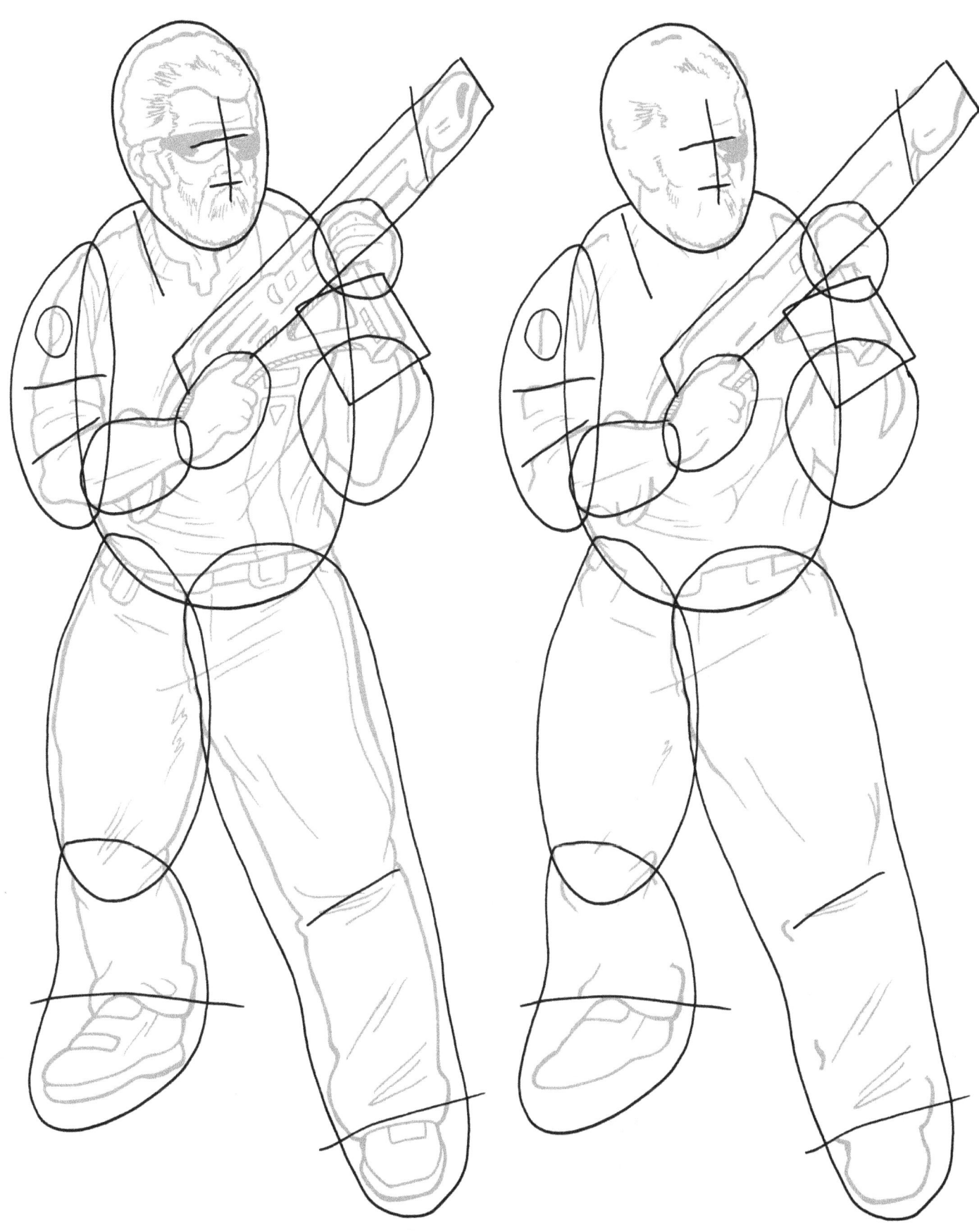

23

Now copy the picture into the blank shape grid. Take your time—you can do this.

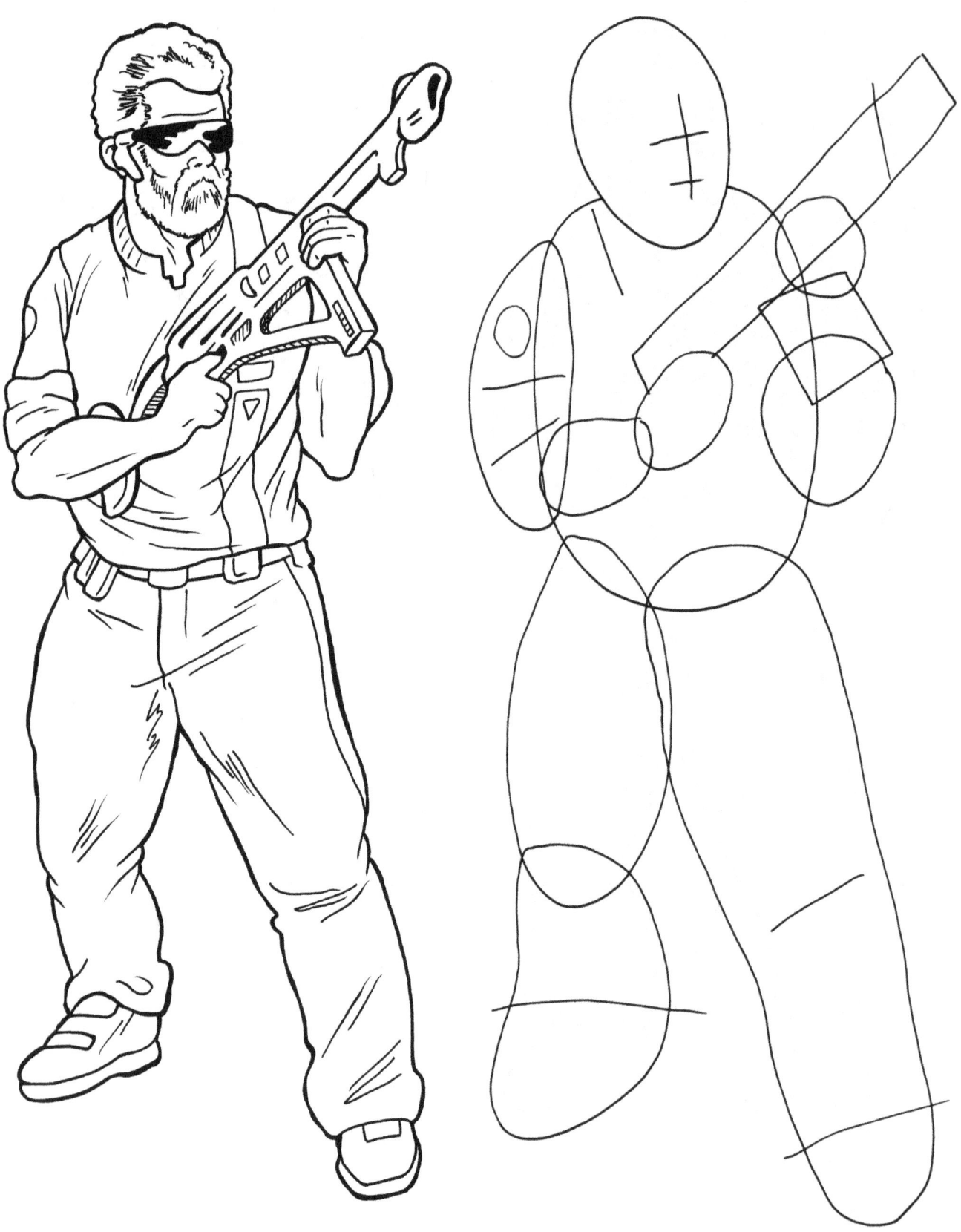

24

Return of the stick people

You know those stick people you've been playing with (you have been drawing your stick people, right)? Well, they're back. Only we're going to modify them a little.

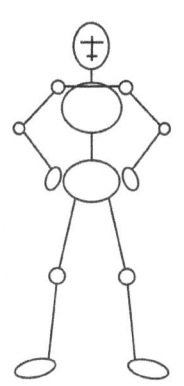

Where the eyes would be we're going to add a line. Where the nose would be we're adding a line through the center of the head. And, finally where the mouth would be we add a line. Everywhere we have shoulders, elbows and knees we add a circle (note the line that connects the two shoulders). For now the hands and feet will be ovals, but when we have fingers you'll want to add a line for each of those.

Just as you looked for shapes that closely matched what you were copying, now you're going to draw a stick person to match the drawing as closely as you can.

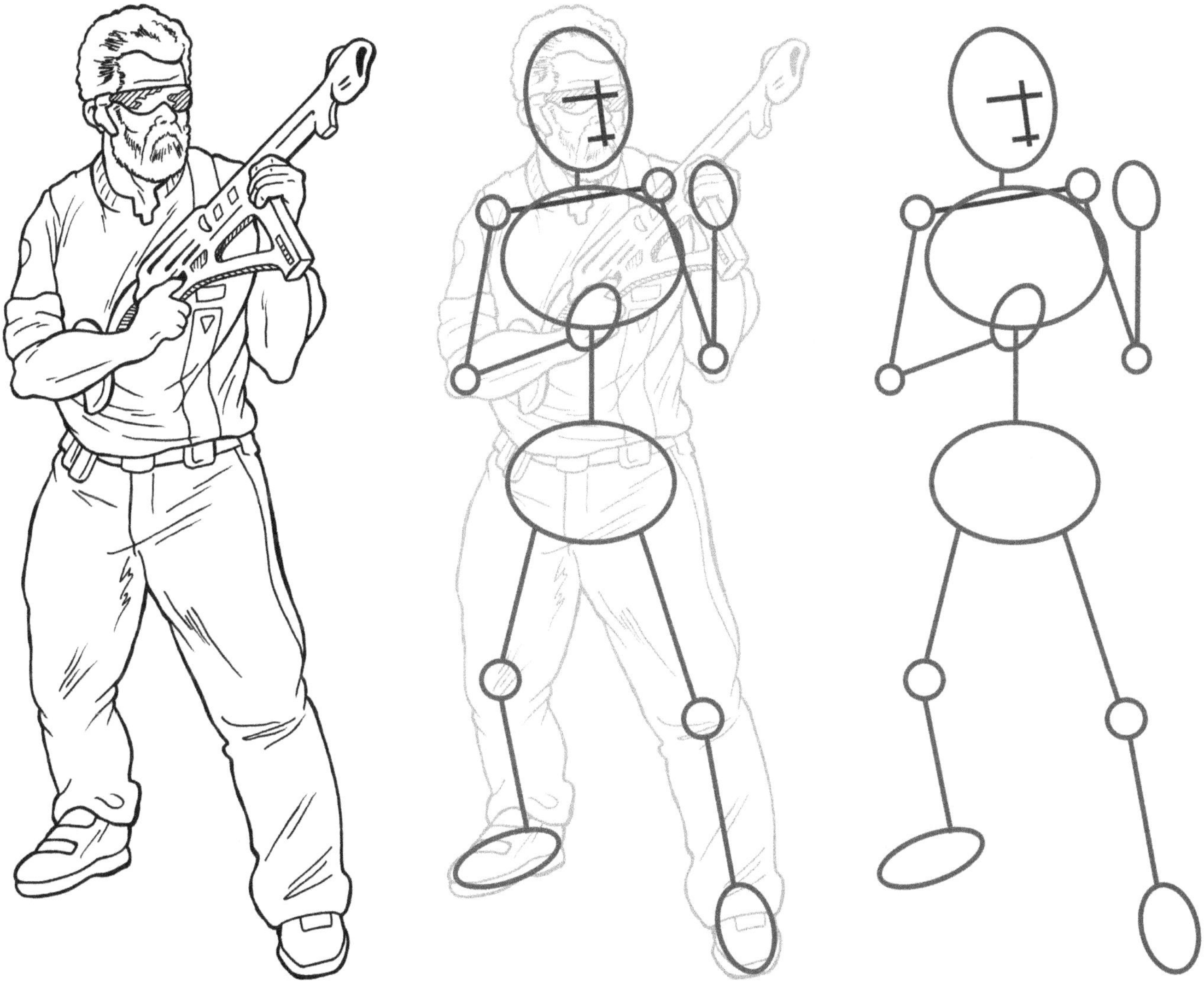

And—just as you did with the shapes—once you have the guide to work from, copy the picture by drawing the picture in sections. First the head—use the eye, nose and mouth lines to help you get everything where it should be. Then draw the neck and shoulders...one arm and then the other—until you have successfully copied the entire picture. Try this a few times. When you feel it's working for you, let's take it one step further.

Not only can you use the stick people to copy a picture, you can use them to alter the pose of the picture.

Again, use your imagination to find the stick person hiding in your picture. Then, using the skill you developed drawing all those poses of stick people (you did continue those exercises, didn't you?) change the pose and see if you can draw the same character in a different pose. You might be surprised how well you do.

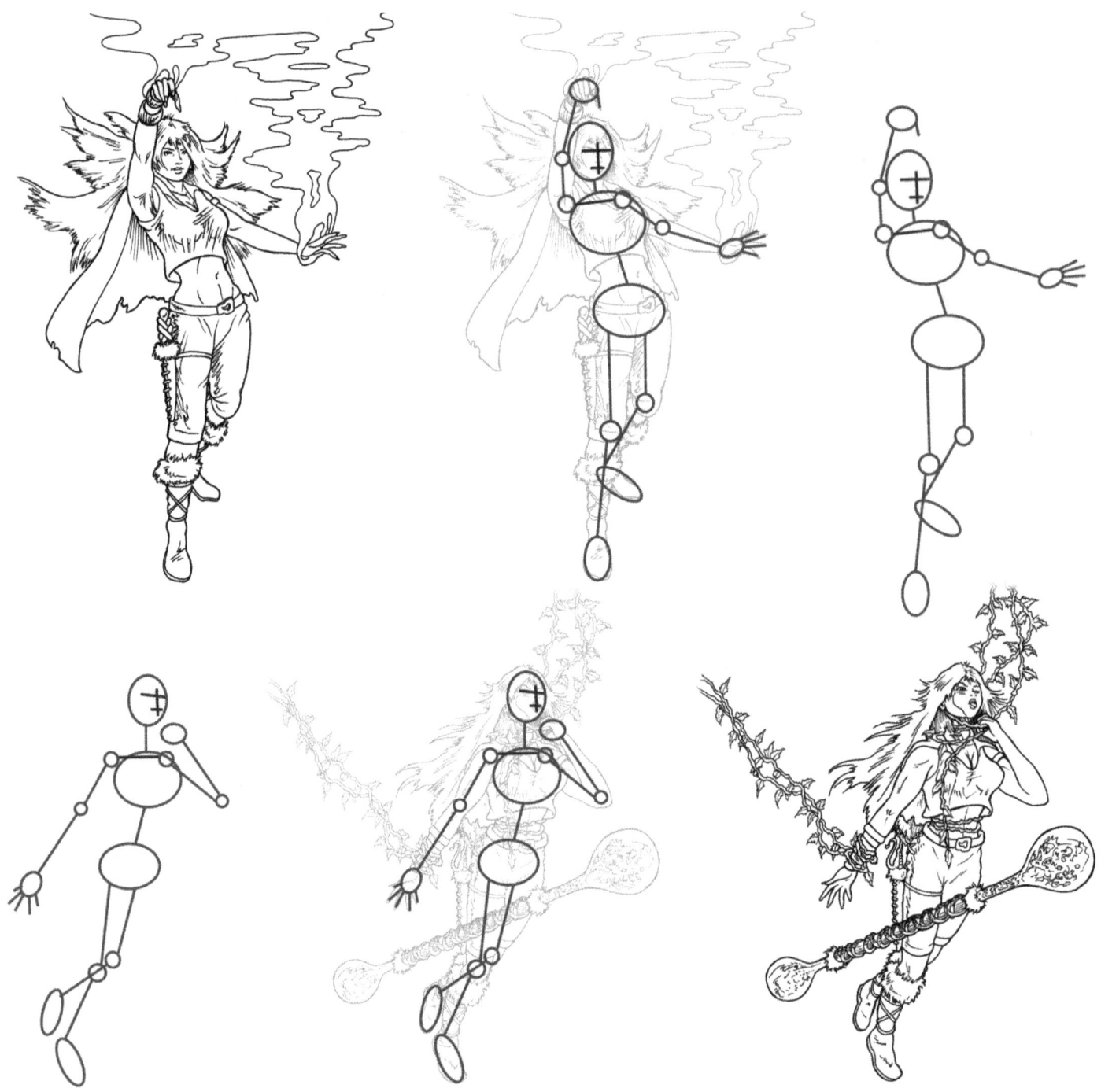

Use the pictures on the next few pages to change the pose of the characters. I've broken it into two parts for this lesson. First copy the one pose and then copy the second. Don't let the different look trouble you—copy the pictures exactly the way you did using the grid or shapes. Only this time, you're using stick figures and then altering the pose. You're still copying parts of the picture, you just have to change what you copy a bit as you transfer the lines from one set of shapes (one pose) to the other. Dig in and use your imagination. I know you can do it!

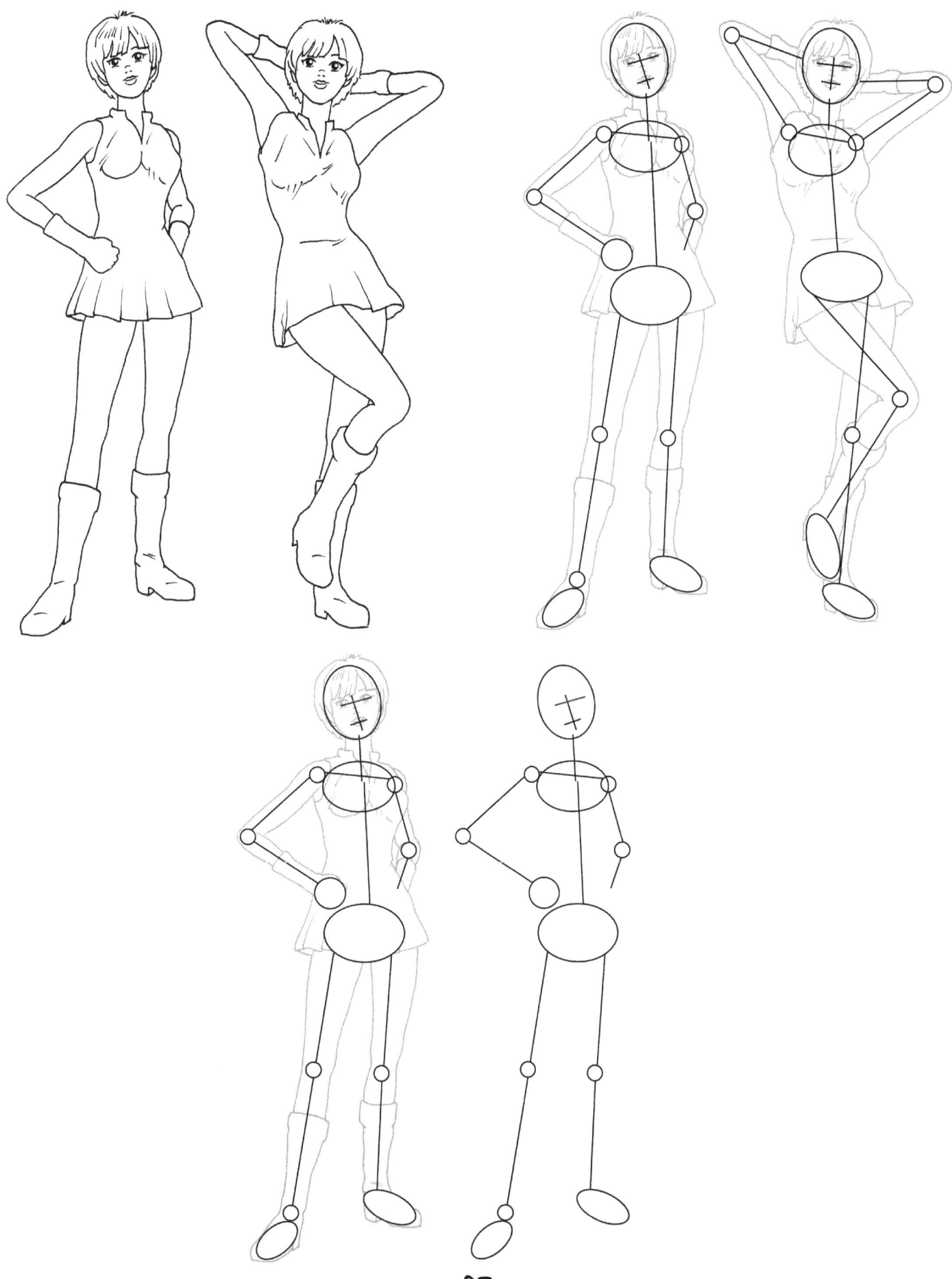

27

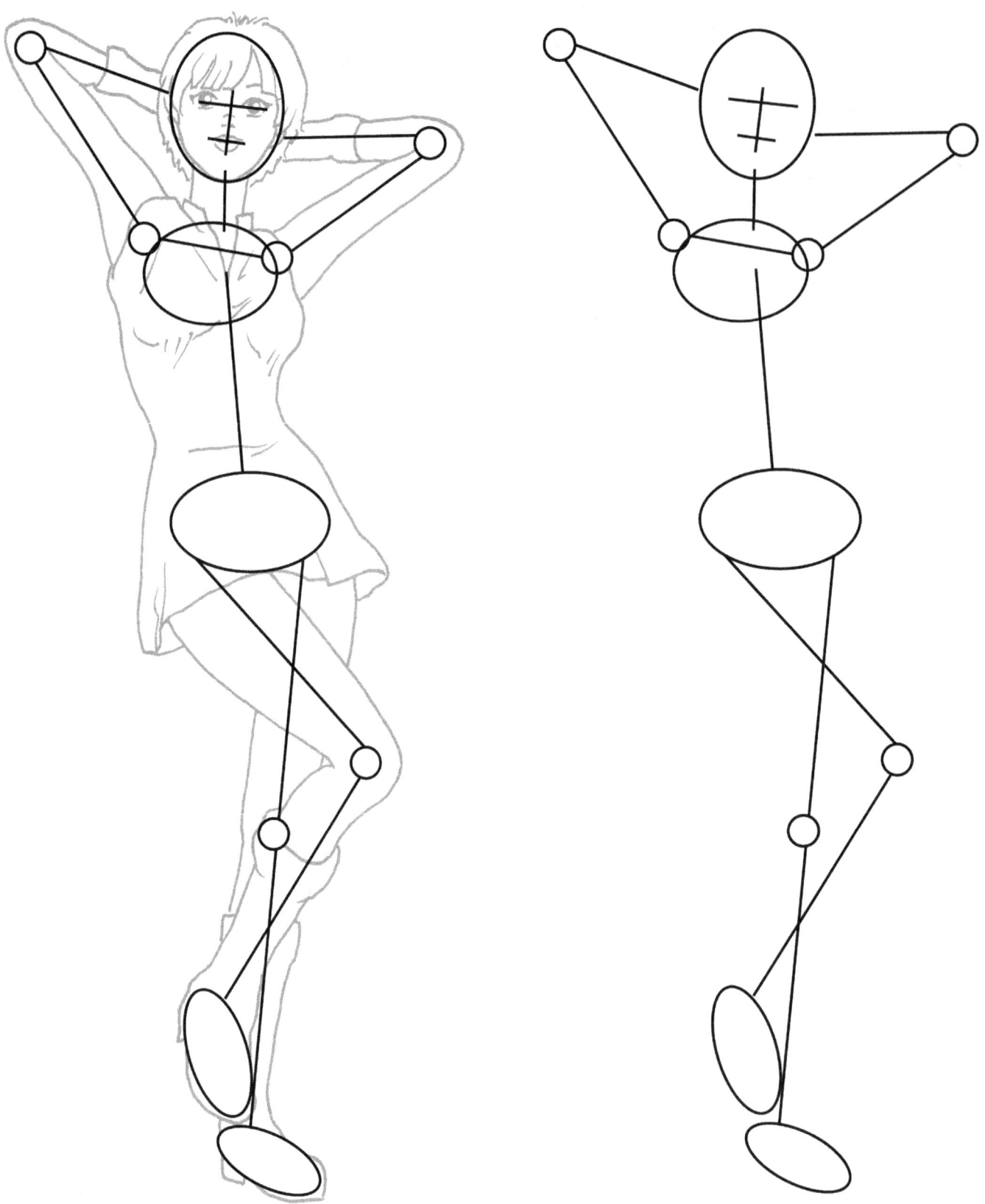

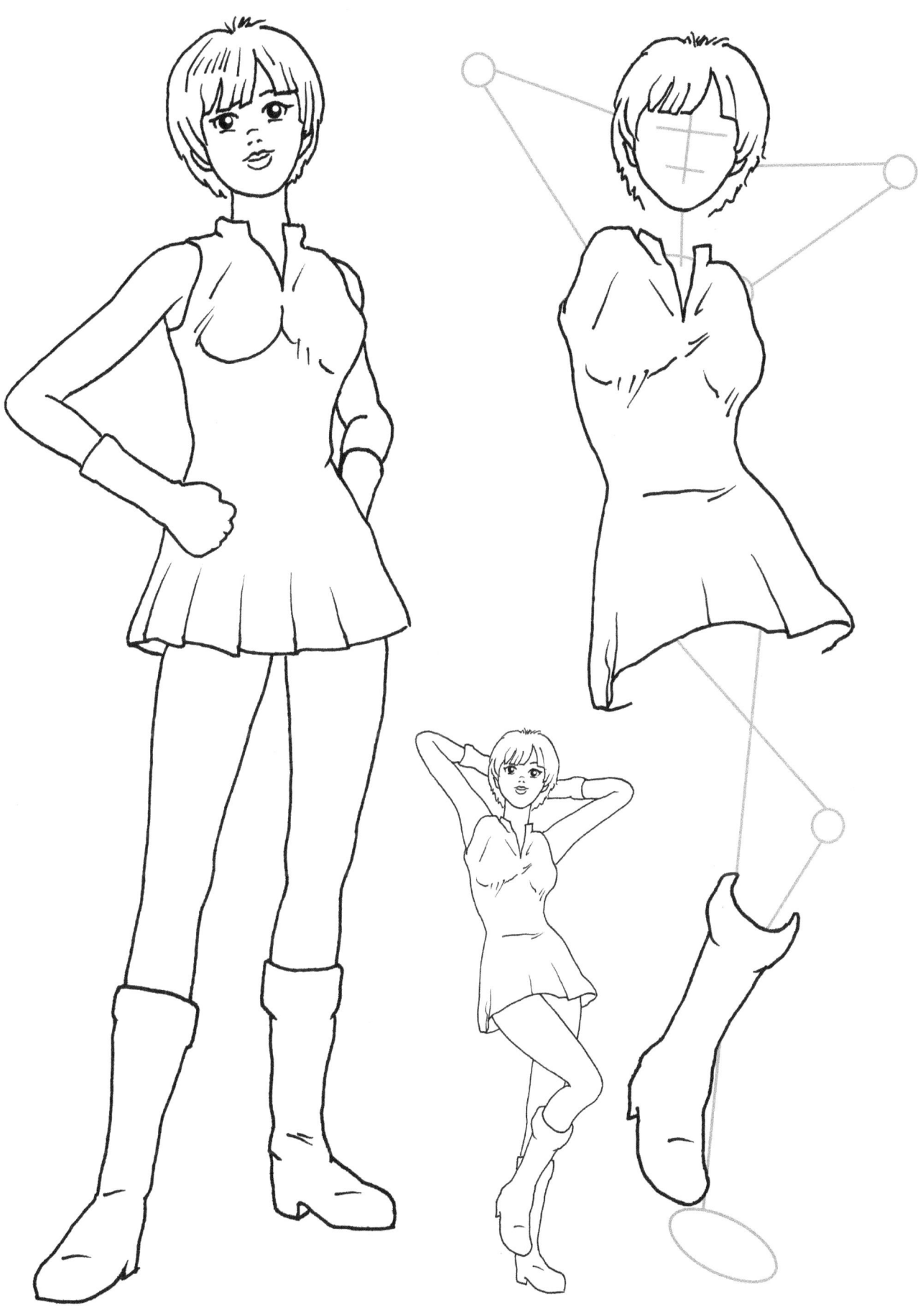

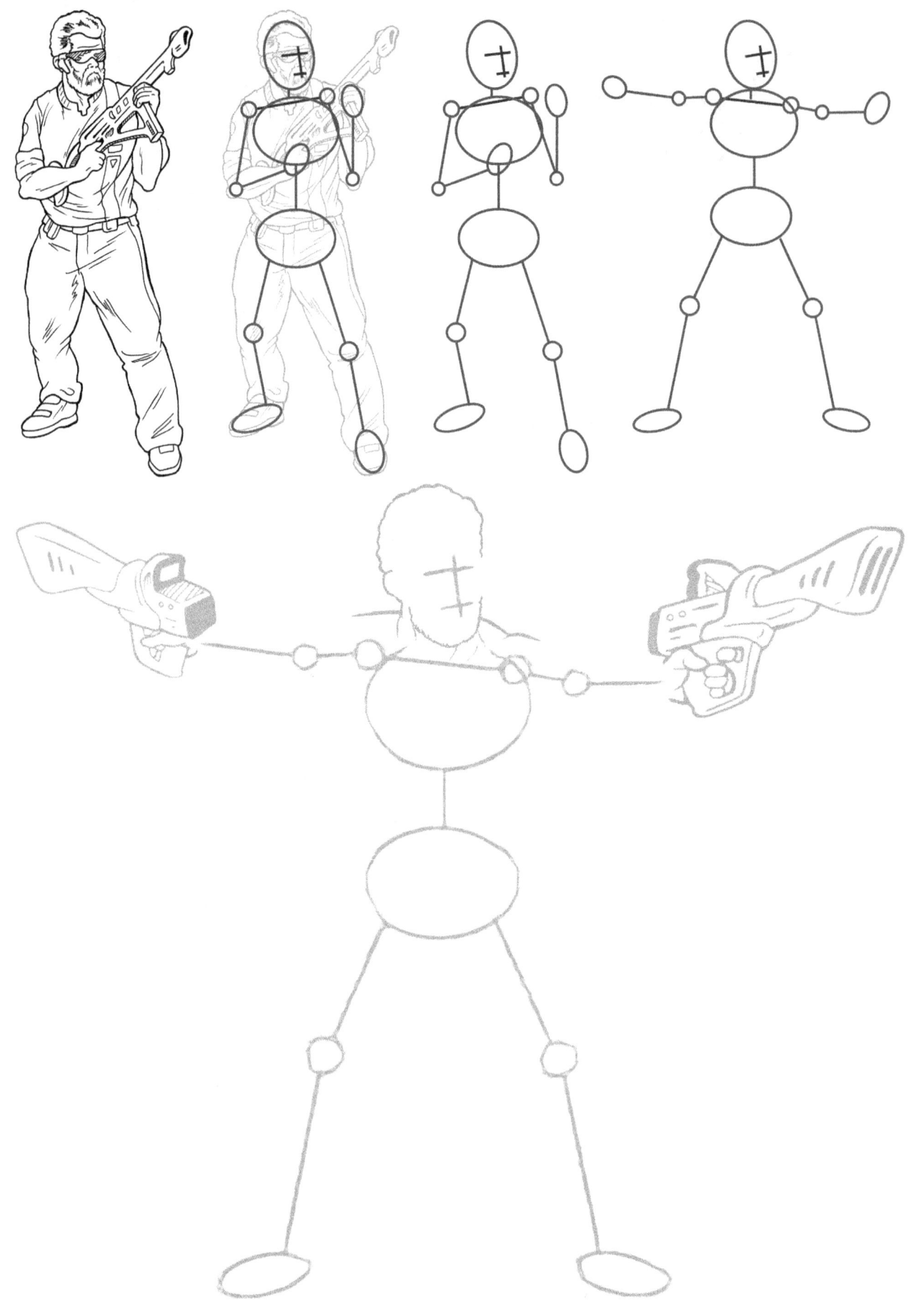

If you're changing the direction a person is looking, try to find another picture with a similar pose as the one you're creating. Check out how that pose creates the eyes, nose, etc. Over time you'll be making those changes without having to look at another picture.

Don't expect perfection—yet—just try to be as accurate as you can. The more you draw the better your work will look.

Once you are finished with this picture, try a few more. If you can successfully change the pose of a picture you copy, then you will be ready to start creating your own art.

Guess what, you're an artist

Don't get too cocky, you still have plenty of work ahead of you, but when you changed the pose of an existing piece of art, you created an original piece of art.

At this point you are ready to try your hand at drawing original art. You're **stick drawing** is now the **skeleton** to any character you draw. Simply use it to pose what you want to draw. You have been tracing and drawing eyes, noses, mouths, arms, legs, etc. for some time now. Then you took those items and posed them how you wanted them to look. If you have successfully done everything in this book up to this point, you already have what you need to create your own art.

Create your pose using the skeleton and draw in the face and hair. Then add detail to the body. Play with the clothing. You'll make plenty of mistakes, but you should be able to make some drawings you'll be proud of.

When you're not sure how to draw something, look at one of the pictures in this book or any other illustration and see how someone else did it. Plus, you should also study photographs and magazine pictures to see if you can copy their poses and details.

It takes a little imagination and a lot of practice, but once you learn to find the lines in photographs you will improve your art tremendously. If you're having trouble copying real-life pictures, try exactly what you did with line drawings. First trace a lot of pictures. Once you've started finding the lines in the pictures then move onto grids and then shapes. The process is exactly the same.

I also recommend you consider finding other how-to draw books now that you have the basics behind you. The next section lists a few how-to books I like as well as a few of my favorite artists.

A good place to start

Here are a few suggestions to get you started in your quest for art instruction and reference books. Since I'm partial to science fiction, fantasy and comic books, it should be no surprise that my suggestions for books will be books by people in those genres. Consider this to be a good starting point. You'll need to do a little research on your own to find artists and books that better fit your style.

The books listed below have been among my favorite "how-to" books. Artists and art books will differ in what each offers you. It's in your best interest to make sure you check out a variety of books and artists to give you more to pull from as you work on developing your skills. Definitely search for material beyond what I present here.

Draw Comic Book Action *by Lee Garbett* — Remember those stick people you've been drawing? This book does a great job of putting them to use.

How to Draw Comics the Marvel Way by Stan Lee and John Buscema — It's an oldie but a goodie. This book has been around since the late 1970's, but what it teaches is still useful today. This book covers things like using basic shapes to help you create your pictures, perspectives (something similar to your stick figures is used in this book) and other useful tips.

Drawing Cutting Edge Fusion *by Christopher Hart* — Hart is one of my favorite artists for "how-to" books. He does a nice job of simplifying things as he presents them. You may see a few stick people here, too.

Astonishing Fantasy Worlds *by Christopher Hart* — This one's a little more advanced, but I like the way he shows the way to use a modified stick person to help you create the characters.

31

Drawing Cutting Edge Comics *by Christopher Hart* — This Hart book and the next one are a bit more advanced. Once you get used to drawing poses and are ready to move beyond the very basics, these are good books to go to next. The book does a nice job of simplifying the details of your characters.

Drawing Cutting Edge Anatomy *by Christopher Hart* — This book is admittedly a little less impressive than the previous, but it does expand a little beyond Drawing Cutting Edge Comics.

Finally, another artist whose instructional books you'll probably want to check out is ***Andrew Loomis***. His work is very old, but what he has to teach you is just as important as what's in the books I listed above. His books are nice to look at no matter what stage of art you're in, but you'll want to read and work through the first books in my list before attempting his. Though his books are out of print, several are now being re-printed. Look for them on the Internet—copies are usually available.

Fun With a Pencil (1939) *by Andrew Loomis* — This is a good book for beginning artists. Though you may want to start with some of the books listed above first, this one easily fits in the list I gave you. And shapes and stick figures even make an appearance.

Drawing the Head and Hands (1956) *by Andrew Loomis* — This is one of my favorites. It does a beautiful job of breaking down two of the more difficult parts of the body to draw into easier to understand parts.

Figure Drawing for All It's Worth (1943) *by Andrew Loomis* — Probably the most comprehensive of his books—if you don't get any other Andrew Loomis book, you should try to find this one.

Creative Illustration (1947) *by Andrew Loomis* — This book's a good bit more advanced than some and not really for the beginning artist. That said, there's some beautiful art on its pages and the text does give a lot of insight into the world of graphics.

Eye Of The Painter (1961) by *Andrew Loomis* — Another more advanced book for when you decide to move into painting (something I believe you should hold off on until you have experience in illustration). Even though this book is about painting, many of the things he covers are relevant to all art.

Successful Drawing (1951) by *Andrew Loomis* — This book goes from simple for the beginner to complex somewhat quicker than I like, but it is a nice, comprehensive book with many nice tips for artists.

As you go through various art instruction books take note that many of them will have you create shapes connected with lines that should remind you a little of the stick men you've been drawing. Some may also use blocks and/or ovals that might remind you a little of the shapes you've been using for copying art. Though the different techniques won't look exactly like what you've been working with, the idea is still very much the same as when you used the shapes. You'll be using the stick/block bodies to create the poses for your characters and once you have the basic shapes in place, you build on the sketch in much the same way as you copied the art into the shapes. Only here you'll be adding the details from your own imagination.

Study the art of other artists

It's a really good idea to find artist you like and study their work. I have a few favorite artists I have followed over the years. If you're into fantasy art, you'll probably enjoy their work.

Be warned. Many artists consider the human body to be a beautiful thing and want to draw it. They are not afraid to draw/paint nudes. It is very common to encounter nude people in art—especially fantasy art. If the person studying here happens to be a teenager or younger, it would be wise to include their parents in the material being collected.

A favorite artist of mine is **Frank Frazetta**. Though his art isn't necessarily the most realistic, it does tend to be incredible and the action in his work is unmatched. You can usually find a good sampling of his art on the Internet and there are some very nice books that have been printed that showcase his work.

Boris Vallejo has a completely different style than Frazetta. His art has less energy, but he manages to get a much more realistic and emotional element to his art. Some of his art (and honestly not usually my favorite pieces) does tend to be a bit sexual in nature. But the life he brings to his art makes it worth exploring.

I had the privilege of meeting **Keith Parkinson** before he died and also got to see a good number of his original paintings (not prints). There's something special in seeing original art and his work was wonderful. His art lacks a little of the life that Frank Frazetta and Boris Vallejo manage to put in their work, but the details to every part of his art is amazing. He would photograph things like old trees and rocks that he found interesting and work them into his art to make the background as interesting as the characters he put in the foreground.

Larry Elmore's work falls somewhere in between Boris Vallejo and Keith Parkinson's while still being something different than both. I've had the opportunity to meet Larry Elmore as well. He's a very nice gentleman and always willing to offer advice to aspiring artists. His art has a little less action than Frazetta's and a little less emotion than Vallejo's. His backgrounds aren't quite as detailed as Parkinson's. Yet the life and detail he brings to his work makes it equal to theirs, just different.

Though it may sound like I am comparing the artists listed here, that is not my intention. Each one of these artists has a completely different style and set of skills. By finding artists' art you enjoy and studying their work, you open yourself to more options and have a greater likelihood of being successful with your own art.

How about comic book artists? These days there are a great number of amazing artists in the comic book world. Since I started into comic books years ago, my favorite artists tend to be some of the older ones. I'll just list a few at the top of my list.

John Byrne admittedly isn't great compared to some of the talent out there, but he managed to produce a lot of nice art regularly that had a nice balance of detail and emotion. He could tell a story very well and that is really the number one thing a comic book artist (in my opinion all artists) should be concerned with.

George Perez's art brings an element of realism and detail to the comic book world. Though the life in his characters isn't as developed as some other artist's work, the beautiful detail in his work certainly added enough life to the comic book to more than make up for it.

Frank Miller's work is interesting and definitely worth studying. I once had a teacher who told me Stephen King is one of the worst writers published (I'm not sure I agree, but this helps me make a point). That teacher also told me there wasn't a professor who taught literature in the department that could start reading one of his books and be able to put it down. His incredible ability to tell a story greatly outweighs any shortcomings in his grammatical skills. Frank Miller is pretty much the same to the art world.

There are easily better artists out there than Frank Miller—yet I can't think of anyone who tells a better story with their art than he does. He's a very good storyteller and whenever he writes a comic book illustrated by someone else it turns out well. But many of the best comic books you'll find are the ones Frank Miller both writes and illustrates.

Todd McFarlane brought a different view to comic book art. It crossed some imaginary line between realistic and cartoonish. By taking realistic art and exaggerating it in a very cartoonish manner he creates a level of emotion and action in his comic books that had not been done before.

Along the same lines as McFarlane, but in a very different style **J. Scott Campbell** has emerged perhaps as my favorite comic book artist. His art has a playfulness I like while being able to deliver action and emotion when needed. There's a detail and beauty to his art that moves him to the top of my list of favorites. For some of his best work, check out Danger Girl — the Ultimate Collection by J. Scott Campbell and Andy Hartnell.

Immerse yourself in art

When the time comes that you begin creating your own original art, do what I do—immerse yourself in art—or, more accurately, surround yourself with art. Find art that you like from different artists and place it around you so you can be inspired by it all while you draw. The art doesn't have to be of the same theme as you're working on, it just needs to be art that you enjoy. However, you can also use the art to help you create a theme. If you're working on a fantasy piece you might have lots of castles, horses, knights, dragons, etc. If you're working on science fiction art you may want stars and planets, robots, rockets—anything that gets you in the mindset to work on science fiction.

More important than themes is that you find art that you like. In order to create your best work you have to want to draw and it helps to be a little inspired. And don't rule out your own work as part of the collection you surround yourself with. If you have art you created that you are happy with, that can help greatly in motivating you to get creative.

Portfolio

When you create art, make sure you keep it together and near you. You may wish to keep your tracings and copied art separate from original art (once you begin to create original art), but you should always maintain a portfolio. At some time in the future you may wish to use your portfolio to show others what you have created, but for now it will be a very useful tool to help you keep track of your progress—thumb through it occasionally to see how you're improving and what you might do to continue to improve.

Luck is not a factor

Many years ago, as I followed my high school band director into his office to try out for a position in the band, someone wished me "good luck." The band director stopped, turned around and said "luck is not a factor." Though he said it with a very serious face, I knew there was a sense of humor behind his statement. That moment has stayed with me all these years. He was an amazing man and the great success of our band was due to his hard work, his inspiration that made us work harder and his never leaving anything to luck.

I had planned to end this book with a simple "good luck" somewhere in the closing, but I'm not sure that luck is a factor. If you go through these pages slowly—not moving on to the next section until you are ready—and dedicate the time and effort needed, you have all the elements you need to start a successful path in art. Talent is always a plus in art, but a desire to draw and a willingness to dedicate the needed time to develop skills can get you just as far as natural talent.

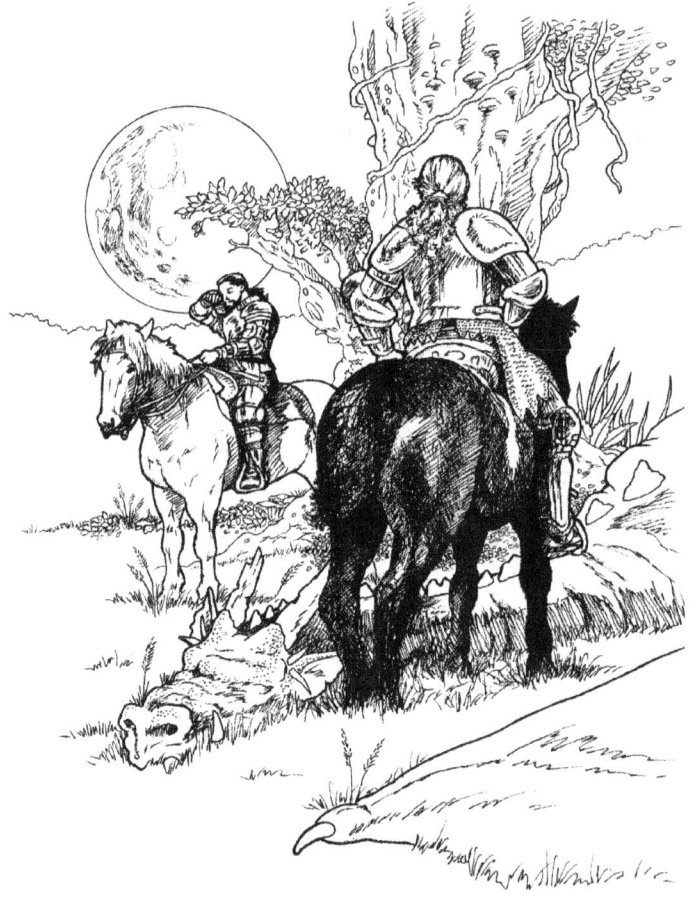

If you truly wish to draw, use this workbook as it has been set up and then continue your studies either with the books I recommended or instructional books more to your liking.

So, here's wishing you much success and—oh what the heck—good luck.

Work Page

Work Page

Work Page

Work Page

Work Page

Work Page

Work Page

Work Page

Work Page

Work Page

Work Page

Work Page

	A	B	C	D	E	F	G	H	I	J	K	L
1												
2												
3												
4												
5												
6												
7												
8												
9												
10												
11												
12												
13												
14												
15												
16												
17												
18												

	A	B	C	D	E	F	G	H	I	J	K	L
1												
2												
3												
4												
5												
6												
7												
8												
9												
10												
11												
12												
13												
14												
15												
16												
17												
18												

	A	B	C	D	E	F	G	H	I	J	K	L
1												
2												
3												
4												
5												
6												
7												
8												
9												
10												
11												
12												
13												
14												
15												
16												
17												
18												

	A	B	C	D	E	F	G	H	I	J	K	L
1												
2												
3												
4												
5												
6												
7												
8												
9												
10												
11												
12												
13												
14												
15												
16												
17												
18												

	A	B	C	D	E	F	G	H	I	J	K	L
1												
2												
3												
4												
5												
6												
7												
8												
9												
10												
11												
12												
13												
14												
15												
16												
17												
18												

	A	B	C	D	E	F	G	H	I	J	K	L
1												
2												
3												
4												
5												
6												
7												
8												
9												
10												
11												
12												
13												
14												
15												
16												
17												
18												

	A	B	C	D	E	F	G	H	I	J	K	L
1												
2												
3												
4												
5												
6												
7												
8												
9												
10												
11												
12												
13												
14												
15												
16												
17												
18												

	A	B	C	D	E	F	G	H	I	J	K	L
1												
2												
3												
4												
5												
6												
7												
8												
9												
10												
11												
12												
13												
14												
15												
16												
17												
18												

	A	B	C	D	E	F	G	H	I	J	K	L
1												
2												
3												
4												
5												
6												
7												
8												
9												
10												
11												
12												
13												
14												
15												
16												
17												
18												

	A	B	C	D	E	F	G	H	I	J	K	L
1												
2												
3												
4												
5												
6												
7												
8												
9												
10												
11												
12												
13												
14												
15												
16												
17												
18												

	A	B	C	D	E	F	G	H	I	J	K	L
1												
2												
3												
4												
5												
6												
7												
8												
9												
10												
11												
12												
13												
14												
15												
16												
17												
18												

	A	B	C	D	E	F	G	H	I	J	K	L
1												
2												
3												
4												
5												
6												
7												
8												
9												
10												
11												
12												
13												
14												
15												
16												
17												
18												

	A	B	C	D	E	F	G	H	I	J	K	L
1												
2												
3												
4												
5												
6												
7												
8												
9												
10												
11												
12												
13												
14												
15												
16												
17												
18												

	A	B	C	D	E	F	G	H	I	J	K	L
1												
2												
3												
4												
5												
6												
7												
8												
9												
10												
11												
12												
13												
14												
15												
16												
17												
18												

About the Author

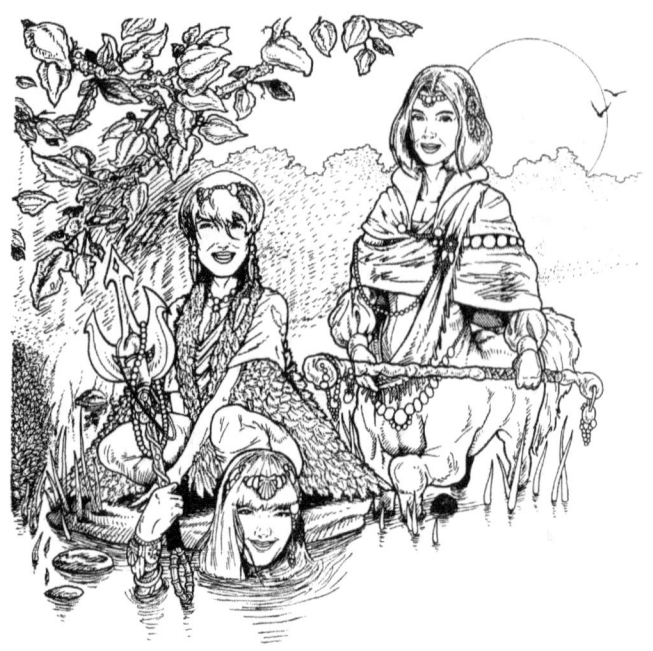

Steven Moore has been telling stories with his art since he was a young child. Though he has worked professionally as an artist ranging from screen printing and ad specialties to computer graphics and design, He has always taken time to create science fiction and fantasy art for fun.

Author Candace Sams wrote: "In Steven's artwork, I see the whimsy, intensity and honor of each character he has imagined. Every pen stroke has been placed with not only an eye to detail, but to draw the onlooker into a place and time many of us wish existed.

"It's easy to see he loves his work. His black-and-white renderings are of such quality that anyone studying them can imagine another reality. If you scrutinize his art for any length of time, you can actually smell the greenery of magical woodlands; hear the clank of armor, or the whinny of a high-bred stallion. Listen closer and you can hear the smattering of gnome voices as if they're beside you. When a dragon roars, Steven captures the sound of it with ink.

"What Steven has shared isn't just the talent of drawing. He's conveying dreams. And in a world that is often tormented with despair, tragedy and cynicism, there is no greater gift one human can give another then the ability to imagine. The worlds he creates—with his pens and inks—are stunning and full of life. And all this from a human being who is as humble and friendly as some of the ethereal characters he has crafted.

"It would be enough to say that Steven Moore is a master artist, skilled in mesmerizing others with his fantastical drawing. But add to that his ability to magnificently write stories to go with the characters he sketches and it's easy to see some otherworldly force is acting through him. Truly... the gnomes, elves, dragons and knights are on Steven's side. Through him, they become real to the rest of us. Through him, they speak to us all."

Born in Frankfurt Germany on a U.S. Army base, Steven Moore has traveled to several countries and been to numerous states within the U.S., but has lived most of his life near the Gulf Coast of Alabama. He currently resides in Loxley, Alabama with his wife and daughter.

His *Runes & Realms* series is the first of the *Downtime Reads*™—books written for the entire family to enjoy during their downtimes and specifically written to motivate mid-grade readers and reluctant teen readers to read.

To encourage anyone who wishes to draw, but feels they can't or don't know where to start, he created the *How-To Book for Artists Who Can't Draw*. A workbook for the true beginner.

He is a proud member of *The INSCRIBABLES:* a group of successful writers a who have teamed up to educate, inform and inspire the creative young.

Visit the *Grim Trojan* site featuring the work of Steven Moore: **www.grimtrojan.cor**

Check out the *INSCRIBABLES* at **inscribables.grimtrojan.com**

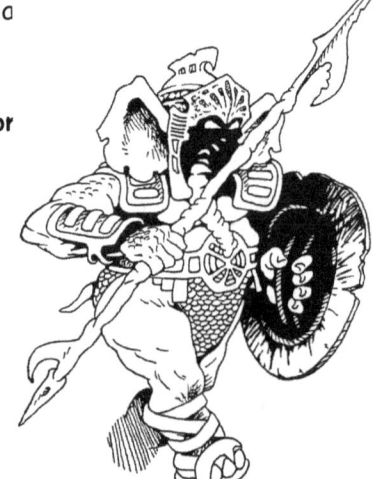

www.ingramcontent.com/pod-product-compliance
Lightning Source LLC
Chambersburg PA
CBHW081827170526
45167CB00007B/2746